⚔ STORIES FROM ⚔
MONTANA'S
ENDURING FRONTIER

EXPLORING AN UNTAMED LEGACY

JOHN CLAYTON

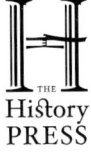

Published by The History Press
Charleston, SC 29403
www.historypress.net

Copyright © 2013 by John Clayton
All rights reserved

Front cover, top: Four men in "dude" cowboy attire stand in front of a bar in downtown Billings, Montana, in 1939. The disparities—"frontier" outfits in front of a neon sign, and silk "cowboy" clothing now more ornamental than functional—illustrate the continuing influence of the frontier in twentieth-century Montana history. *Library of Congress LC-USF33-003092-M3. Bottom:* A view eastward down the Swift Current Valley, a former mining district now mostly reserved in Glacier National Park. *Kari Clayton photo.*

Back cover: Haydie Yates bridged dude and cattle ranching cultures, then wrote a captivating but now-forgotten memoir. *Photo courtesy Angus Yates. Background:* Grasslands around the old mining town of Bearcreek. *Kari Clayton photo.*

First published 2013

Manufactured in the United States

ISBN 978.1.62619.016.0

Library of Congress CIP data applied for.

Notice: The information in this book is true and complete to the best of our knowledge. It is offered without guarantee on the part of the author or The History Press. The author and The History Press disclaim all liability in connection with the use of this book.

All rights reserved. No part of this book may be reproduced or transmitted in any form whatsoever without prior written permission from the publisher except in the case of brief quotations embodied in critical articles and reviews.

to Kari

Contents

Author's Note   7

I. Places and People
In the Bighorn Canyon   13
The Best Kind of Cowboy Hero   20
Montana's Carnegie Libraries   24

II. Outlaws
An Urban Army   35
Fame and Bandits   42
The Trials of John L. Smith   48

III. Economies
Camp Senia and Montana's Dude Ranching Heritage   55
Origins of the Beartooth Highway   62
Hope and Bacon   70

IV. Communities
Mossmain: Montana's Near-Metropolis on the Plains   77
Community, Enriched by Formula   84
In the Garden of Eden   90
The Teenaged West   97

CONTENTS

V. FRONTIERS
Wister's versus Turner's Frontier — 103
Disney's New Western Frontier — 106
What We Do on Today's Frontier — 109

VI. THE NEW WEST
All-Harley Cowboys — 115
The "New West" Is an Old Concept — 118
Ten Years and Counting on a Meaningless Phrase — 121

VII. AUTHENTICITY
A Permanent State of Not-Quite-Decay — 125
Vacation to the 1830s — 131
Clarence Mulford's Odd Western Journey — 136
A Regular He-Man Horse — 139

VIII. HEROES
The Mountain Man Who Outshone His Legends — 145
Resurrecting Haydie Yates — 150
At the Little Bighorn — 157
The Native Home of Governors on Horseback — 165

Acknowledgements — 171
Index — 173
About the Author — 176

Author's Note

When it comes to the history of Montana and the American West, I say enough with the Indian fights, vigilantes, and cattle drives. What I find compelling is when places start actually filling up with people, such that those activities necessarily fade. In this phase, like a teenager coming to grips with what kind of person he or she is going to be, the region starts developing a personality—one that shapes its future.

As Montana's frontier faded, Montanans started building communities. Of course, there had always been communities in the vaguer sense of the word: links among groups of Native Americans, trappers, soldiers, prospectors, or far-flung ranchers. But physical communities—towns and cities each with an economic and social and architectural structure—could arise only when there were enough people to both need and create them. So what did that process look like in Montana? What dreams did the state's natural splendor inspire? How often did those dreams succeed, how often were they further elevated into myth, and how often did they collide with hardscrabble reality to hone the character of everyone involved? That's what I'm always writing about.

Montana didn't run out of frontier all at once. Along the Butte–Miles City railroad corridor (see p. 35), it was vanishing in the 1890s. In the imagined metropolis of Mossmain (see p. 77), the post-frontier age was going to arrive about 1914, but then evaporated. And when I visited a particular spot in the wilderness outside Yellowstone National Park in 2002 (see p. 109), the frontier there seemed to be cantankerously thriving.

Author's Note

Thus, one of the great things about Montana is the way its frontier endured for much of the twentieth century. This untamed legacy created a patchwork, in marked contrast to other places. Consider, for example, Illinois. When sufficient numbers of Illinois' homesteads were claimed, forests cut, fields plowed, savages tamed, and fortunes made, the frontier exited Illinois, stage left. In 1840, Illinois was primarily wilderness; by 1860, it was the fourth most-populous state in the Union. And so Illinois advanced. Like teenagers grasping that they will not go into the family business, the burgeoning Illinois communities moved on to more intensive agriculture, processing plants, factories, or whichever other activities best suited their strengths.

In Montana, however, "stage left" was already taken, and there was no place else for the frontier to go. Sure, there have been claims that "the last frontier" boldly goes to Alaska, or space, or the Internet. But the traditional view of frontiering (see p. 103) doesn't necessarily follow, instead fading unevenly into Montana's background.

And so, unlike so many other states, as Montana ran out of frontier, Montanans intensified their relationship with it. Indeed, many residents even defined their vacations or communities by it (see p. 131). In part, of course, that's because Euro-American history is so new on this ancient land. It feels more immediate. In part, Montana lacks Illinois' moisture-rich soils, navigable waters, and central location. Like a teenager entering the job market during a recession, Montana lacked options to move on to. And in part, the word "frontier" has come to take on a variety of pleasant meanings: triumphant rural simplicity, a hardship-bred physical and spiritual strength, peaceful naturalism, social naiveté, the chance to make a lot of money. Focusing on a disappearing frontier allows Montanans to do more than pursue dreams—it allows us to simultaneously pursue apparently contradictory dreams, and do so while seeing ourselves largely in harmony with our neighbors. Although some observers might call that "refusing to grow up," I think it's a pretty neat way to live a life.

THIS BOOK EXPLORES what happened when Montana ran out of frontier. And rather than a plodding who-when-where of development, it investigates the question through a variety of narratives, portraits, and perspectives. Although it is, for me, the culmination of twenty-plus years of writing about Montana history, I was not really aware of being on a journey. So to the extent this book serves as a journey for you, I hope you can dawdle, pause,

Author's Note

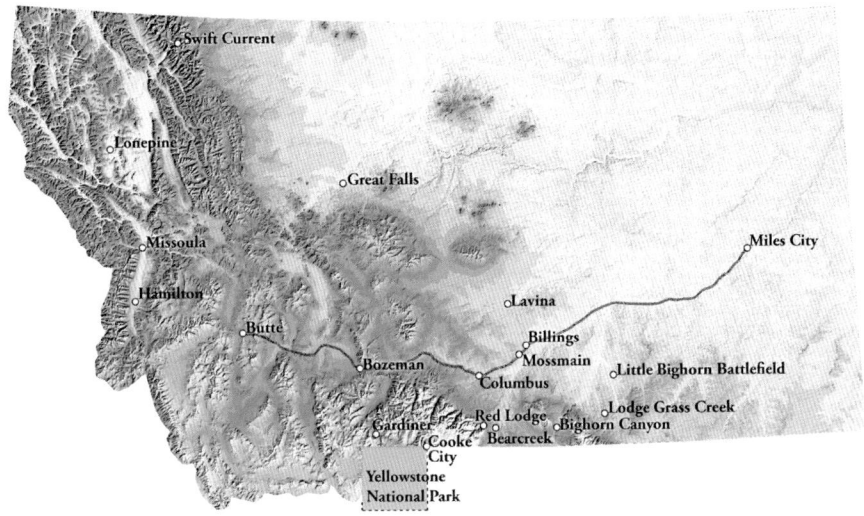

Some of the locations of the stories contained in this book. *Map by Kari Clayton.*

doubt, double back, and otherwise stimulate, question, and enhance your own view of Montana and its history.

A few structural notes: I've chosen to organize the book by grouping together similar impulses or developments or types of characters. Because these essays were written over a long period, I have simply indicated the date (and, where relevant, the original publication) at the end of each. Although a woman named Caroline Lockhart makes occasional appearances here (because no compilation of my research and writing could avoid such a fascinating character), there is no overlap between this book and my full-length treatment of her life and times in *The Cowboy Girl*. Finally, although I have dropped all footnotes from this book, for readability, I would be happy to share sources with scholars (contact me through www.johnclaytonbooks.com).

At times, compiling these essays has made me feel strange and vulnerable. Am I really publishing a sort of Greatest Hits collection? Did I really poke into so many corners and issue so many opinions? Seeing them all collected may imply an author more self-assured, ambitious, and even dogmatic than the way I like to think of myself. Yet at the same time these are stories—about wonderful characters, such as John "Liver-Eating" Johnston (see p. 145), or quirky programs, such as The Montana Study (see p. 84)—that I have particularly enjoyed writing and sharing with people. I'm pleased to have a chance to make these stories available in this format, and I hope you too may find some favorites in here.

Part I

PLACES AND PEOPLE

In the Bighorn Canyon

I have come to think of Bighorn Canyon as "I had no idea" country. That's mostly because when I tell people about its Lake Powell–like cliff-and-water landscapes, they say, "I had no idea it was there." It's also because even those of us who do know it's there are continually surprised when we explore.

I've been visiting the southern end of Bighorn Canyon—in the far eastern reaches of Carbon County, east of the Pryor Mountains, but accessible only by driving north from Lovell, Wyoming—for seven years now. I've been working on a biography of Caroline Lockhart, who in 1926 homesteaded a ranch in the rugged badlands above the canyon. A small thrill of my drawn-out research has been bringing visitors from out of town, telling them we'll visit the site that inspired the book.

I don't tell them what we'll see nearby: wild horses, a driftwood-filled lake, or the thousand-foot cliffs that hide it. So on the long drive through the barren landscapes of Wyoming's northern Bighorn Basin, punctuated only by oil derricks, bentonite mines, and a sugar-beet processing plant, I can tell they're wondering how this unearthly journey would be worthwhile. Then we come to the Devil Canyon overlook and it all spreads out below them.

The canyon was one of the last major continental rivers to be explored by Euro-Americans. When Edward Gillette left Crooked Creek on March 7, 1891, he knew only that the Bighorn was a box canyon with rapids and falls, that nobody had ever run the river, and that a few had tried and perished. (By comparison, though large areas of southern Utah remained unexplored for longer, John Wesley Powell had run the Colorado River itself twenty-two years previously.)

Gillette made his descent in winter so that any hidden rapids or waterfalls would be covered with ice. But even so, by the time he reached the northern end of the canyon, he was almost too late. The ice extending across the narrow canyon floor was so thin that he attached a rope to the lightest member of his party, who "squirmed over the undulating ice while I let out the rope, ready to pull him back should he break through."

Gillette, an accomplished adventurer, found this trip most worthwhile. He wrote, "The Grand Canyon of the Colorado is an immense chasm, so broad as to reveal a wide valley. The Royal Gorge of the Arkansas River is magnificent for a short distance only and the stream is small, while the Yellowstone canyon is awe-inspiring and gorgeously colored for a comparatively brief space. The Bighorn canyon, however, combines all these features with that of a true box canyon and such features as overhanging cliffs that are not to be found elsewhere."

LIKE MOST CANYON landscapes, Bighorn geology is a story of a stubborn river sticking to its course. When these lands were flat, the Bighorn took a meandering path north to the Yellowstone. But centuries of erosion eventually exposed a thick deposit of Madison limestone. Limestone is relatively water-soluble—and indeed both the Pryors and the canyon walls are pockmarked with caves—so the meanders cut down through it quickly. Later, the river encountered other layers of rock, but the seven hundred feet of Madison is what makes for dramatic cliffs.

That and a lack of rainfall. With just six to ten inches of rain a year, the erosion of the canyon walls is much slower than that powered by the river. It's like digging a ditch: in mud, the sidewalls would keep falling in, creating a wide, shallow depression. The lack of water keeps these sidewalls vertical. It also reduces vegetation that could hide the dramatic story of bare rock.

Meanwhile, the Pryor and Bighorn mountain ranges rose on each side of the canyon. The Pryors, in particular, were lifted along a steep vertical fault plane, so from the Devil Canyon Overlook you see Madison limestone a thousand feet above you as well as a thousand feet below. But limestone is not the only rock in play here: it's occasionally capped with a brilliantly red Chugwater siltstone.

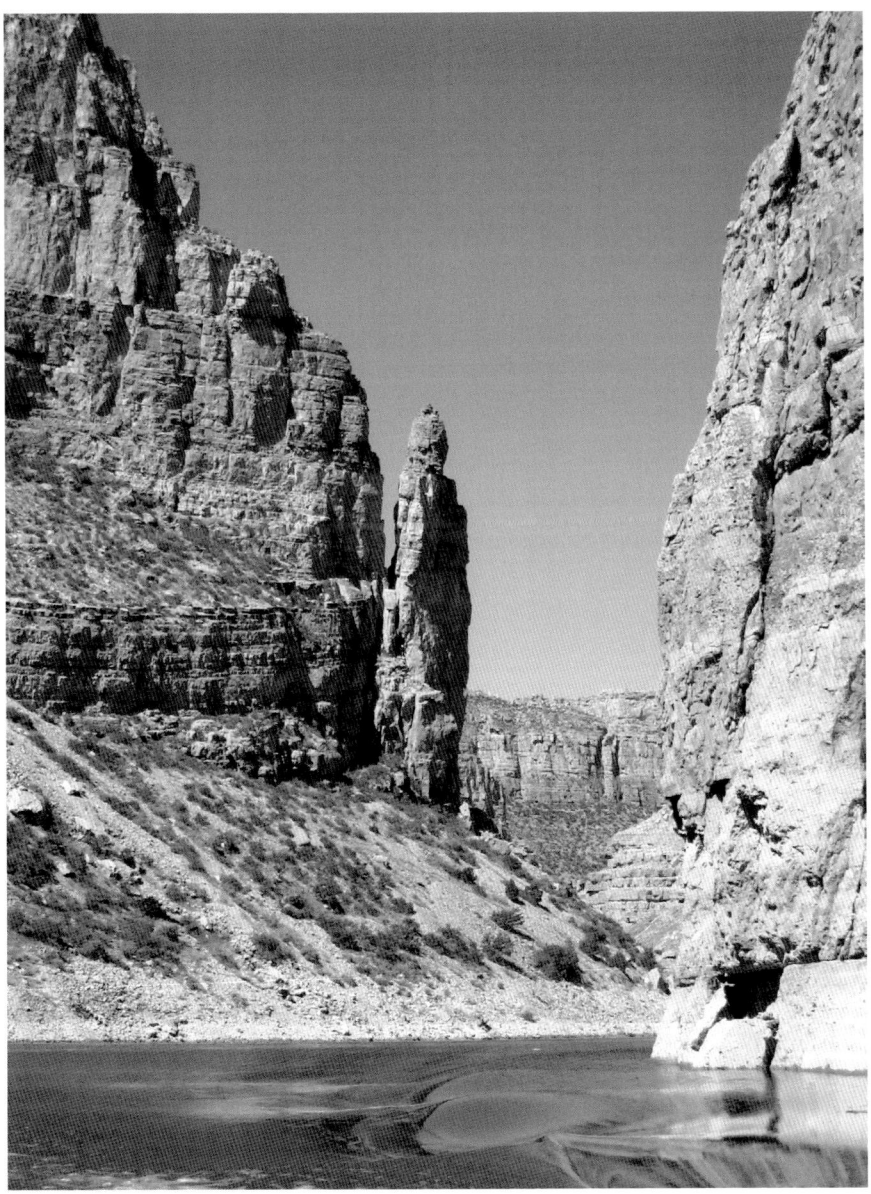

With its forbidding Madison limestone cliffs, the seventy-one-mile-long Bighorn Canyon was one of the last in the continental United States to be explored by Euro-Americans. Even today, access is difficult except by powerboat. *Courtesy Kari Clayton.*

Siltstones—especially combined with the lack of rainfall—make a poor basis for agriculture, which has contributed to this region's longstanding lack of development. Though indigenous hunter-gatherers created the Bad Pass trail parallel to the canyon ten thousand years ago, and mountain men used that trail during the fur-trading era, there were few permanent settlements in the area before 1900.

Indeed, though Gillette found no significant waterfalls to impede summer traffic, little such traffic ensued. Unlike the ancient river, humans found easier ways to bypass this rugged country. Rail lines and roadways developed east of the Bighorns and west of the Pryors. With prospectors finding few precious resources, agriculturalists barely scraping by, and most of the land north and east of the canyon belonging to the Crow Indian reservation, the area remained remote.

In 1967, the federal government built Yellowtail Dam at the north end of the canyon, near Fort Smith on the reservation. The dam backed up the river for seventy-one miles, turning Bighorn Canyon into Bighorn Lake, a National Recreation Area managed by the National Park Service. In a sense, the dam made the canyon more accessible than ever—as long as you had a powerboat. But the lake is still a long way from any population center.

In June 2007, my friend Greg Shanks, a Red Lodge semiprofessional walleye fisherman, took a group of us out on a boat tour. We put in at Barry's Landing, the end of the paved road from Lovell, about halfway along the lake. It was only my second time on the lake and my first time there on a powerboat, able to fully explore the canyon's expanse.

Greg first took us south, to Devil Canyon below the overlook. I'd had some idea of how impressive the thousand-foot cliffs would be, since I'd seen them from above. But I had no idea how stunningly imposing they would feel from below, my view constrained to lake, cliff, and a tiny patch of sky.

Nor had I any idea how much driftwood there would be on the lake surface, or how strange it would feel to be surrounded by huge waterlogged tree trunks—and no live trees. Many of the trees fall in the mountains and are carried down tributaries to the lake—which, this June, was at its highest level in years, floating such debris to the surface.

The lake's level can vary by as much as sixty feet, a circumstance that recent drought has turned into a political issue. In some recent years, the lake has never even risen high enough to open boat docks at Barry's Landing or Horseshoe Bend (with the latter being further hampered by siltation). Yet as Lovell-area recreationists and businesses call to hold more water behind the dam, fly-fishing fans ask for steady releases from the dam to maintain the outstanding trout habitat of the river below Fort Smith. More precipitation might make both parties happy, but without it no easy solution exists.

We stop to do some fishing, and Greg tells some stories of his years visiting the lake. I had no idea that an area so sparsely vegetated could be so wonderfully laden with wildlife. The road to Barry's Landing goes through the Pryor Mountain Wild Horse Range, and driving it remains one of the easiest ways to spot those special creatures. But Greg talks also about elk, bighorn sheep, and mountain lions, often coming all the way down to the bottom of the canyon. Indeed, he once even saw a black bear swimming across the lake.

We head back north, and I marvel at the length of the canyon. It goes on and on, the cliffs sometimes lowering to a few hundred feet but then soaring back up. They rarely recede from the lakeshore, which contributes to the stunning verticality but also makes it difficult to land a boat. There's lake, and there's cliff—few beaches, willows, or other attributes we associate with a "streamside." Two developed areas that do have such attributes, Black Canyon (to the north end of the lake, near the dam) and Medicine Creek (near Barry's Landing), get a lot of use. As Greg describes the crowds that can overwhelm these spots on a summer weekend, I tell him I had no idea that some of the busiest campsites in a hundred-mile radius would be utterly inaccessible by land.

Today, however, while exploring a side canyon, we discover an undeveloped landing spot. We get out to eat lunch and explore up the tiny creek on foot. It's a fascinating little ecological back alley, with sage, juniper, cottonwood, grasses, and wild roses mixed with the reddish rock and muddy water. We see raccoon prints and a vein of chalky white substance in the cliff, probably gypsum. We walk no more than half a mile, often in the middle of the two-inch-deep stream, sometimes on rock, and once—as my wife prepares to scramble up a mini-waterfall—in almost eighteen inches of sucking, slurping mud. Greg, who on previous visits has rarely stopped fishing long enough to do such exploring, is impressed. Neither of us had any idea this was here.

Through the afternoon, we continue north to the Ok-A-Beh Landing near the dam, where we refuel before retracing our path back to Barry's Landing. As we proceed, the rock in the cliffs folds and changes color. So does the water: white, brown, and blue-green, all in the same lake.

I'm especially impressed by the way sound carries. I first notice that you can hear an oncoming powerboat coming around a corner long before you

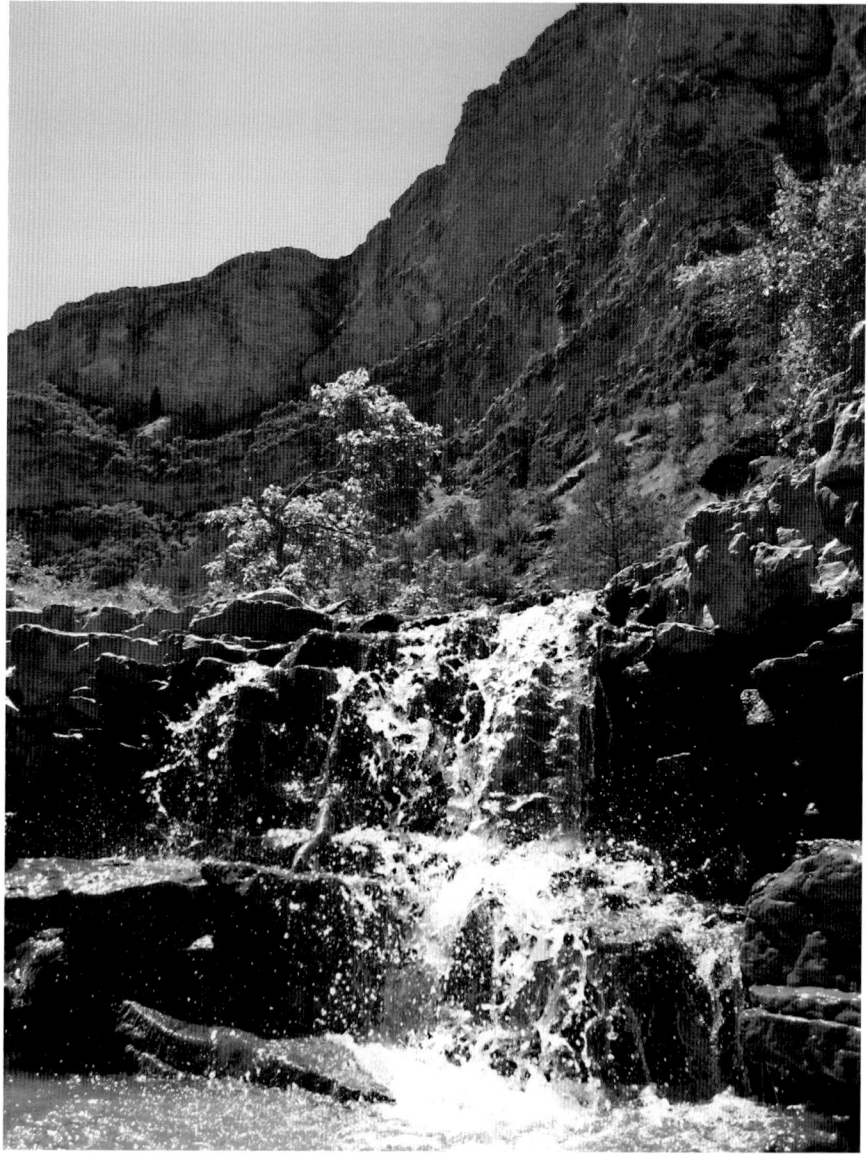

Exploring a side canyon off Bighorn Canyon leads to a rare landing spot and a tiny creek watering an ecological back alley. *Courtesy Kari Clayton.*

can see it. But as we head up the ever-narrowing canyon of another side channel, mergansers make a more impressive version of the same effect. Their sound carries across the water to a canyon wall and bounces back, echoing and filling the space to its brim.

As the day wears on, I continue to be impressed at the canyon's expanse. I've seen it on the map—where it's hard to believe such a meandering path could carve such a steep chasm—but trying to cover the canyon's entire length in a single day is a surprisingly tiring experience.

We barely have time, at the end of the day, to drive three miles beyond Barry's Landing to the little-visited Lockhart ranch. The wet weather that has raised the lake level has also preserved the lush, almost neon spring green of Lockhart's former oasis. Cottonwoods arch over the hewn logs of the main ranch house. Nearby, an old outhouse leans into some willows, and grasses climb up rail fences surrounding the old corrals. You can't see the canyon itself from here, but there's still plenty of strikingly beautiful Madison limestone in the form of palisades along the east front of the Pryors. The sun is low in the sky, and the ranch exudes a sense of peace. I always hate to leave this place, and I'm pleased to discover the others feel the same way.

Again it's a spot Greg has never visited. He nods his head in acknowledgement of what has drawn me to the Bighorn Canyon country. "I had no idea this was back here," he says, and I grin in appreciation of the region's refrain.

Montana Quarterly, 2007

THE BEST KIND OF COWBOY HERO

Another Charlie Russell painting sold for over $1 million in 2003. *Trail of the Iron Horse*, a 1924 watercolor, depicts Indians on horseback puzzlingly encountering a railroad track that runs straight west to the sunset. In 2001, Russell's watercolor *A Disputed Trail* had sold for a record $2.1 million. "That was two people bucking horns at an auction," said the Coeur d'Alene Art Auction's Bob Drummond, and given the burst of the Internet bubble, he hadn't expected a new record Russell.

Regardless, however, it appears that eighty years after his death, Charles M. Russell (1864–1926) is more of a hero than ever. Deservedly so, I say.

Unscholarly scion of a wealthy St. Louis family, Russell came west as an adventure-seeking teen in 1880. He found his adventure cowboying on the big cattle spreads of central Montana, where he also started sketching.

His reputation began with an illustrated letter he sent during the disastrous winter of 1886–87. Titled *Last of the 5,000*, his sketch of an emaciated cow demonstrated two hallmarks of his future work: an emotionally evocative depiction of cattle ranching and a strong sense of storytelling.

Russell soon gave up roping cattle for painting, and his success and fame grew through his life, aided by a business-savvy wife whose first step was to get Charlie to stop trading paintings for drinks.

My first encounter with Russell came on my first adult visit to the Rocky Mountains. My friend Mary, a Wyoming native, called him an ultimate Western figure. I figured she admired his cowboy hat, cowboy skills, and cowboy art. But as she spoke, I realized that what she really admired were

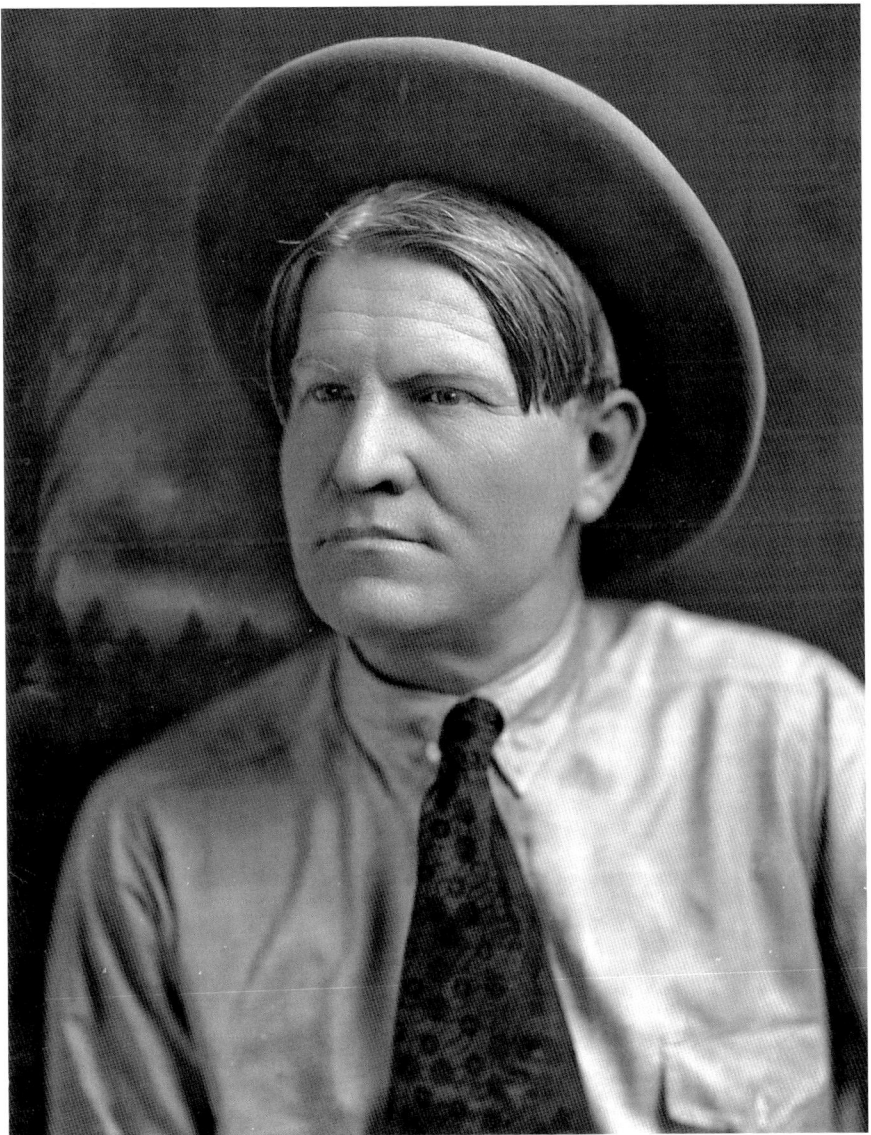

Charles M. Russell, shown here in about 1907, is a hero as an artist, storyteller, and human being. *Wikimedia photo.*

his stories. Always a great yarn-spinner, Russell achieved increasing success in later years writing down his stories with an accompanying illustration. Additionally, throughout his life he illustrated letters to friends—some of these are now his most cherished works.

His storytelling and humor also come through in his subject matter and titles, such as the image of a cowboy approaching a female artist, *She Turned Her Back on Me and Went Imperturbably On with Her Sketching*, or the collection of braves looking down on a boat in the river, *Indians Discovering Lewis and Clark*. Like all the best humor, Russell's brought a new perspective and a hint of melancholy that gave his subjects a deep humanity.

So like other heroes of the Old West, such as Buffalo Bill Cody, Russell's fame comes not so much from his doings as his stories—in this case, ones he both drew and told. He may have worked a few years as an honest-to-goodness cowboy, but his accomplishments accumulated in the city of Great Falls.

That makes for something of a disconnect: A cowboy artist who quit cowboying. A rural artist who painted from a downtown Great Falls studio. A figure of the Old West whose popularity crested after the turn of the century. An artist who magnificently captured the plains of eastern and central Montana but who spent his later summers in a forested-lakeside cabin in Glacier National Park. He even retired to Los Angeles in the 1920s, a decision that his biographer John Taliaferro wrote had a logic "as perverse as it was consistent: First he had built a house in the least Western of Montana's cities; then he had built a summer cabin in the least cowboyish quarter of the state; now he had chosen to spend his winters in the least nostalgic city in America."

But of course we don't honor Russell for the thematic integrity of his life. We honor him for the art that brings strength and beauty to a vision of most young people's dreams. His 1880s images capture nostalgia for the open range, and if one wants to fault him for romanticizing it, one must also fault the rest of the world, which shares that passion.

Russell's paintings are alive with affection, humor, play, and awe. (His contemporary Frederic Remington, meanwhile, tended to focus more on violence.) Especially when we remember that Russell had no formal training, it becomes obvious that Russell's art was fully an expression of his character. It's a remarkable achievement: regardless of the form—watercolor, illustrated correspondence, or memoir—his character shines through. Furthermore, that character turns out to be gentle, honest, forthright, and playful. If Russell is indeed the ultimate Westerner, I sure am glad I live here.

You can learn a lot about a culture by examining how it defines heroes of other eras. So as we increasingly admire the cowboy Charles M. Russell, I am delighted to note that "cowboy hero" need not be associated with violence, taciturnity, or even horsemanship.

Charlie Russell was a man who pursued his passion, who never boasted of killing any Indians (or anyone else, for that matter), and whose idea of a perfect day was to play around with his art for a few hours, have lunch with his wife, and then head downtown to swap stories with his buddies all afternoon.

That alone would make him my hero, regardless of how much money his paintings now bring.

Horizon Air, 2003

Montana's Carnegie Libraries

In 1914, when residents of Hamilton examined the "deal" being offered by a rich out-of-state do-gooding organization, they were skeptical. "They didn't want to be told what to do," laughs Gloria Langstaff, director of the Bitterroot Public Library. The gift they were being offered did indeed come with strings. And the strings were likely to bring about a permanent raise in their taxes.

Of course, such sentiments are still common across much of the state—and often justified. But in this case, the deal worked out pretty well. The gift, a library building from Andrew Carnegie, still stands. The taxes, for furnishings, books, and maintenance, proved not too onerous. In that era, seventeen other Montana communities made the same bargain, and most still have an impressive building to show for it.

The building is generally brick, in two stories with high ceilings and thirteen steps marching up to the entrance. Its classical detailing—including a simple formality, the prominent doorway, and often an exterior lamppost or lantern to symbolize enlightenment—suggest an elevated purpose. And inside these old Carnegie Libraries are often some of the friendliest and most knowledgeable folks in town.

In 1848, the thirteen-year-old Andrew Carnegie, a recent Scottish immigrant, couldn't go to school: he had to work in a textile mill to help support his family. The highlight of his week was Saturday afternoon, when a local man opened his shelves of more than four hundred books to workingmen and boys. At the time there was no such thing as a free public-access library.

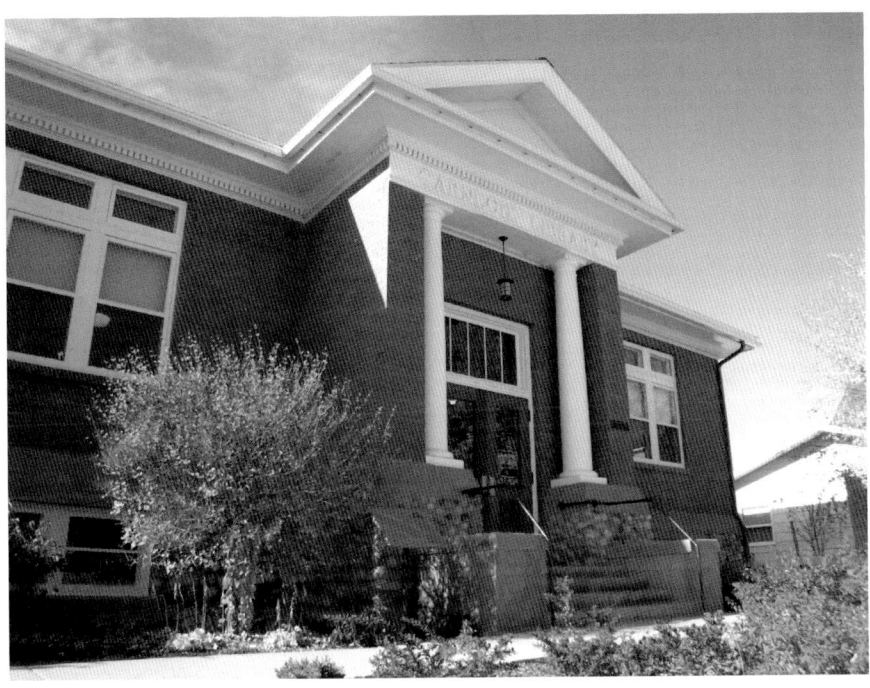

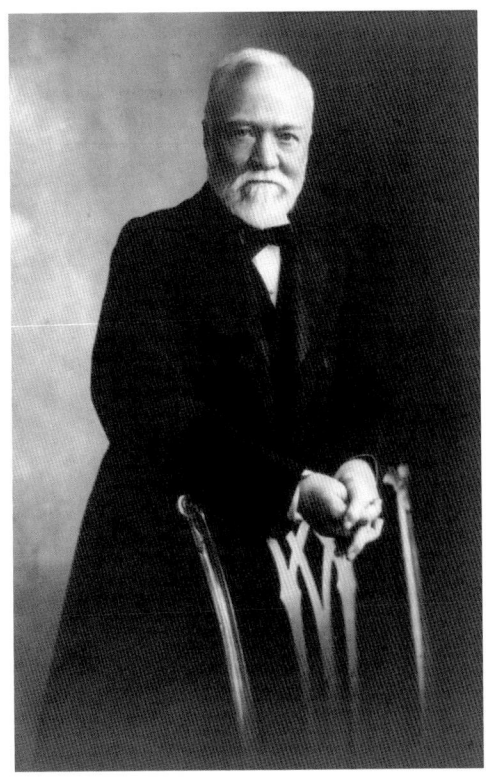

Above: Although Andrew Carnegie allowed architectural variety when he funded library buildings, he did encourage certain features. For example, the Big Timber library includes large windows, classical revival elements such as columns and pediment, and steps up to the entrance to emphasize the way you are elevated by learning. *Courtesy Kari Clayton.*

Right: Industrialist Andrew Carnegie gave away his fortune to build public libraries, including seventeen in Montana. *Library of Congress LC-USZ62-90762.*

Fast-forward several decades: Carnegie became one of the richest men in America, and the idea of the public library started to take hold. The new industrial age put an increased premium on thinking and learning, as demonstrated by Carnegie's own rags-to-riches story. A building where all citizens could go to improve themselves could thus be a physical representation of the United States' commitment to equal opportunity. By 1900, a few hundred such institutions existed in America, but mostly on the East Coast.

So Carnegie vowed to give away his fortune to build public libraries. He would end up providing the money for over 2,500 buildings throughout the English-speaking world, including 17 in Montana.

The timing was perfect: entering the new century, Montana towns increasingly sought maturity and sophistication—culture to go along with a growing economy. In many communities, women's clubs were establishing collections of books to be loaned, but these collections lacked permanent homes. Even in Dillon, where the library did have its own building, townspeople considered it "a miserable wooden shack."

But Carnegie drove a tough bargain. Always the businessman, he considered his gifts to be investments. To be eligible for his money, a community (minimum size: one thousand residents) had to contribute the land for the site and pledge an annual maintenance budget of 10 percent of his donation.

That's what concerned the 1914 residents of Hamilton. Though they eventually relented, their fears may have been prompted by the experiences of Lewistown, where the Carnegie library had opened in 1907 and immediately encountered a financial crisis. Although Carnegie's $10,000 had paid for the building, there was no money for furniture, shelving, electrical fixtures, or even a furnace. So the first year's maintenance budget went to these items—leaving no money for operating expenses. Back when the library had been located in a room of city hall, Lewistown could afford a librarian. But with a new building, there was no money for staff. Volunteers opened the library one day a week, and later that year, a woman agreed to serve as part-time librarian in exchange for free living quarters in the basement.

That sort of arrangement was not what Carnegie had had in mind. He didn't like "multipurpose" buildings; his secretary James Bertram wrote to one Kansas community, "It is all very well for you to plan your building as a dance hall, club, YMCA, dining room, kitchen, etc., but remember Mr. Carnegie is paying for a Library Building and not for this kind of miscellaneous general convenience."

Carnegie and Bertram also had firm ideas about architecture. They favored an open floor plan with bookshelves as room dividers, separate reading rooms for children and adults, and a circulation desk close to the entrance for maximum sight lines. They liked basements to be just four feet below grade, containing lecture, work, and storage rooms as well as a heating plant and toilets. They discouraged elaborate entranceways and fireplaces, saying these took up space that was better devoted to books.

In addition to function, another goal was to make the library one of the grandest buildings in town. As a prominent local institution, a Carnegie library promised to help elevate the lower classes, acclimate new immigrants, and demonstrate a community's permanence. For example, in their applications to Carnegie, Big Timber and Livingston wrote that a library would provide a better alternative than saloons for new immigrants and single men working for the railroad.

The architecture of public buildings at the time was highly influenced by the "White City" of Classical Revival buildings at the 1893 Chicago World's Fair. So most libraries were built in brick or stone, with columns, pediments, arches, and other echoes of Greek temples.

In Missoula, architect A.J. Gibson designed a building in contrasting colors of brick and stone, with a central staircase capped with a pediment and two Doric columns of granite. The city of Dillon chose a slightly different route with Romanesque Revival architecture featuring a steep gable, octagonal tower, and carved faces.

The movement spread like a rumor across the state. For example, the *Havre Plaindealer* reported that the new Carnegie library in Glasgow was "a splendid example of public pride and enterprise and worthy of emulation by Glasgow's onlooking neighbors." And thus Havre soon applied for its own Carnegie grant.

Chinook, in 1918, received one of the last Carnegie grants. Construction in other towns, such as Red Lodge, was delayed by World War I, but Carnegie himself died in 1919, having given away $350,695,653 (well over $4 billion in today's dollars) of his fortune.

As Montana towns grew and changed over the following decades, Carnegie buildings proved outmoded. Indeed, the Missoula library had required a second-story addition in 1913, just ten years after its construction. Many communities' reassessments came in the 1960s, an era when old buildings and classical architecture were not in fashion. In about 1965, Great Falls and Glasgow both demolished their Carnegie libraries to build new ones on the same site, and Miles City constructed an addition

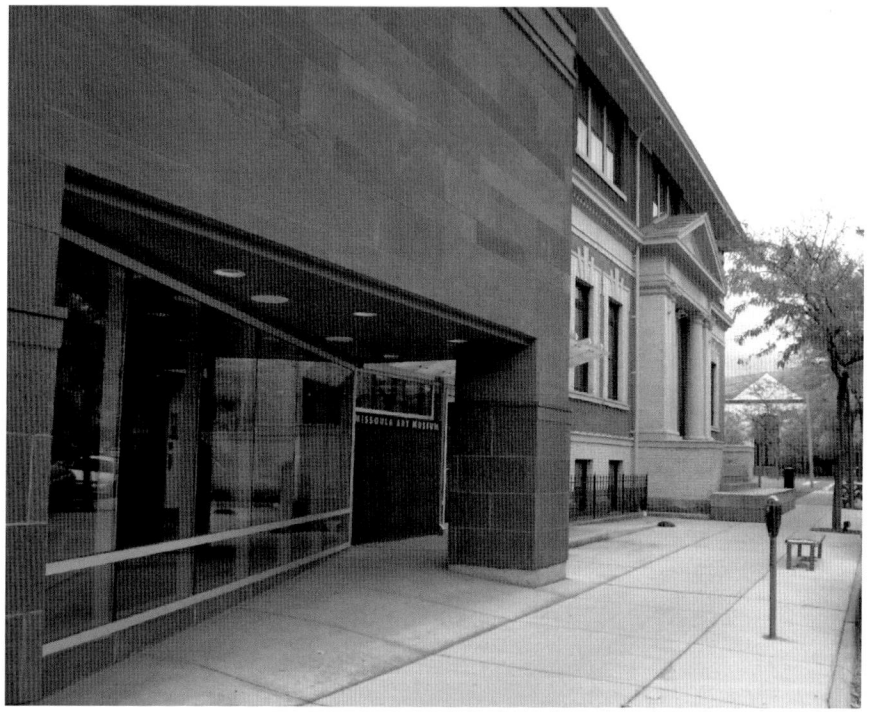

Many communities have renovated Carnegie libraries, sometimes extensively, for new purposes. For example, the Missoula Art Museum, shown here, contrasts the classical Carnegie architecture with a glass-and-stone 2006 addition. *Author photo.*

that wrapped around the front of the building, doubling its size but hiding most of the original exterior.

Issues were not just stylistic but also functional. The thirteen steps—which for Carnegie had been an important symbol of the elevating power of knowledge—made handicapped access difficult. Poor insulation and high ceilings made many buildings expensive to heat. Some lacked parking or room for expansion. Several towns decided to build new libraries, finding an alternate use for the old Carnegie buildings.

Thus several buildings across the state are well known in their current uses but not as old Carnegie libraries. For example, the A.J. Gibson Missoula building is now the Missoula Art Museum, complete with a 2006 glass-and-stone addition. The Hockaday Museum of Art in Kalispell, with its octagonal entrance framed by columns, similarly began as a Carnegie library in 1903.

Kathleen Shirilla transformed the former Havre city library into the Old Library Gallery after the Havre and Hill County libraries consolidated in the old Havre clinic building in 1986. The first floor, with eight twelve-foot-high windows bringing in natural light, displays art, including that of local pencil artist Don Greytak. The lower level of the building, which like many of the other Carnegies is on the National Register of Historic Places, serves as Shirilla's living quarters.

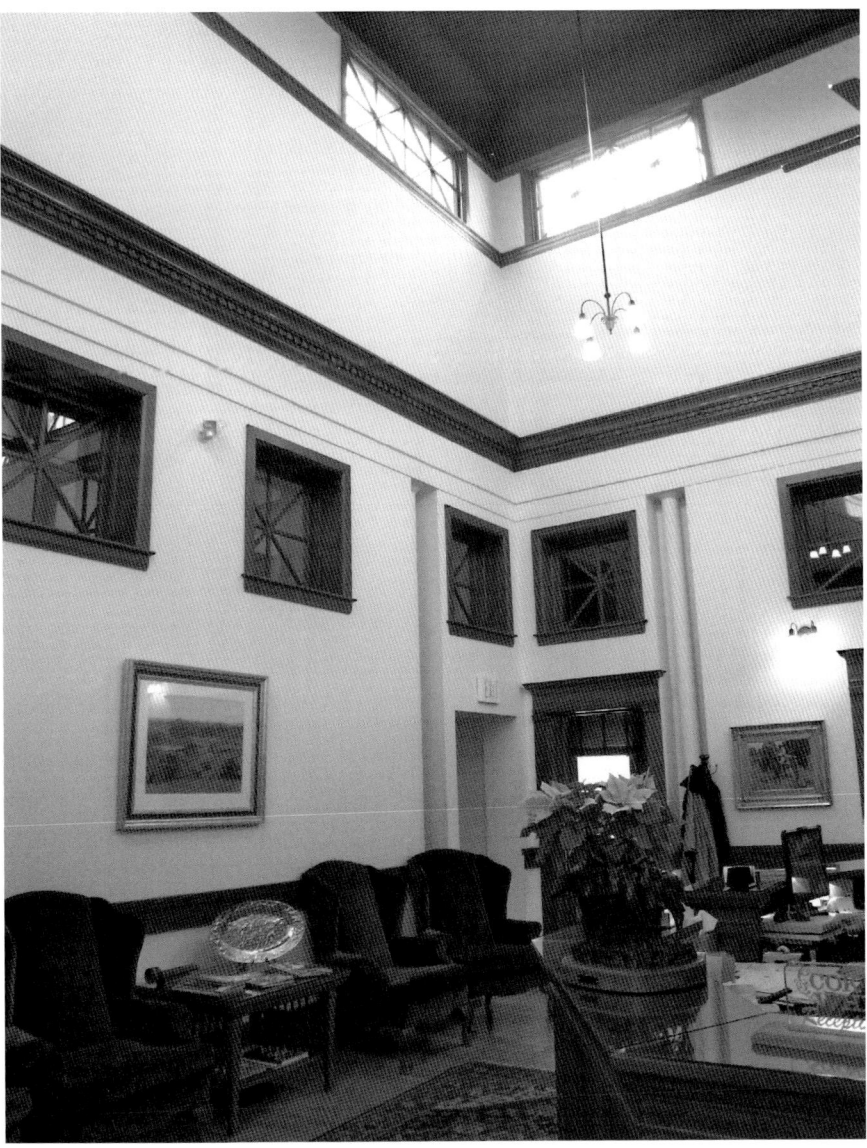

When Bozeman attorney Mike Cok renovated his town's 1902 Carnegie library, he removed a dropped ceiling to expose high windows that bring light to the interior space. *Courtesy Kari Clayton.*

When the original Bozeman Carnegie library was constructed at the corner of Mendenhall and Bozeman in 1902, that was considered the downtown's red-light district. Attorney Mike Cok purchased and restored the building (which had been serving as city offices since 1980) in 1998. The renovation pulled out a dropped ceiling, dating to the 1940s, that had obscured high windows bringing light and elegance to the lobby.

Similarly, the old Chinook library, owned by the school system, is rented to the Bear Paw Cooperative, which manages special education programs in the region. Cooperative director Dick Slonaker says that a few years ago, he decided to investigate what was underneath a series of small, high, boarded-over windows around the ceiling perimeter and discovered that the original windows were in perfect shape. Exposing them, he says, "turned a rather dreary atmosphere into a well-lit, bright, cheerful space."

In Malta, a larger library was constructed in 1979, and the Carnegie building became home to the Phillips County Historical Society. But in 1996, that organization, too, found the library too small for its needs. In 2008, the deteriorating structure was sold at auction to Mark and Tana Oyler. Tana says, "The first thing we did was to stop the roof from leaking. If we were younger, we would have moved right in and started renovating." The Oylers had previously restored three Malta houses while living in them but aren't necessarily up for doing so again at the library. "We just plan to not let it deteriorate any further and hope that someone comes along who wants to maintain and restore some of the beautiful old features of this building," Tana says.

Other communities chose to retain their libraries in remodeled Carnegie buildings. Livingston and Dillon expanded in 1978 (Livingston again in 2005); Hardin, Hamilton, and Fort Benton in the 1980s; Lewistown, Fort Benton (again), and Red Lodge in the 1990s. Big Timber was the final Montana Carnegie building to be renovated, with a spectacular 2007 expansion that tripled the building's size while remaining faithful to its style. "They seamlessly repeated all the original woodwork, the window shapes, and everything," says library director Kate Lewis.

The Big Timber expansion also created a well-used community meeting space. Other expansions have tended to focus on space for both books and study, handicap accessibility, and advanced technology such as computers. Many were funded by local donors. Like Big Timber, Fort Benton retained original furnishings—even old wooden tables and window casings. "The building resembles what it did when it was built in 1918—except for the computers," says librarian Jill Munson.

Libraries have continued to be popular with philanthropists, and seventy-six Montana libraries have received technology grants from the Bill and Melinda Gates Foundation in the past decade. That continuing devotion may arise from the same sentiments one anonymous Montanan shared with Carnegie a century ago: "There is no city so great that it does not wear its library as its chief jewel."

Montana Magazine, 2009

Part II
OUTLAWS

An Urban Army

The old Northern Pacific boxcars overflowed with unwashed, boisterous, and desperate men. Some miles behind them, a trainload of deputy federal marshals was setting off in hot pursuit, and nobody knew for sure when the looming confrontation would arrive. Yet in front of them, at the east end of the Muir Tunnel through Bozeman Pass, the rails were blocked by thirty cubic yards of rock, mud, and timber.

The men, about three hundred of them, had stolen the train. There was no doubt about that. But they believed their cause was just, and the warm welcome they'd just received in Bozeman suggested that many Montanans agreed. But they hadn't counted on these so-called federal marshals, a group instantly deputized from what some people called "the scum of Butte" to do the dirty work of a large and greedy corporation. If that trainload of hired thugs caught these men before they'd cleared the slide, there was no telling what might happen.

Although this may sound like it's building up to the climax of a John Wayne movie, in fact it's a true story. Indeed, it's a surprisingly overlooked piece of Montana history. The three hundred men were part of a nationwide group called Coxey's Army, and their plan was to take part in the first-ever popular march on Washington, D.C.

Problems had started with the Panic of 1893, the worst economic recession in the country's history to that date. Across the nation, banks failed, mines closed, railroads went bankrupt, and unemployment rates soared. And because Montana provided a huge portion of the country's gold, copper, silver, and lead, this state was hit especially hard. By January of 1894, 20,000 Montanans were out of work. At a time when the state's population was just 132,000, the ranks of the jobless may have included as many as one-quarter of all family breadwinners.

In Ohio, a man named Jacob Coxey decided to do something. Though wealthy himself, Coxey believed that men who wanted to work shouldn't be denied the opportunity, so he suggested the federal government initiate a huge road-building campaign. In addition to providing infrastructure, the program would put men to work and stimulate the economy.

To persuade Congress, Coxey urged 100,000 jobless men to present a "petition with boots on" in Washington on May 1, 1894. In late March, he started leading an Ohio contingent by foot.

In addition to being the first-ever proposed march on the Capitol, Coxey's effort was one of the first big national stories to arise in a new era of journalism. Printing innovations and expanding literacy had led, in the 1880s, to new types of mass-appeal newspapers. The papers loved controversy, and for this story they practiced the "yellow journalism" techniques later perfected for the 1898 Spanish-American War.

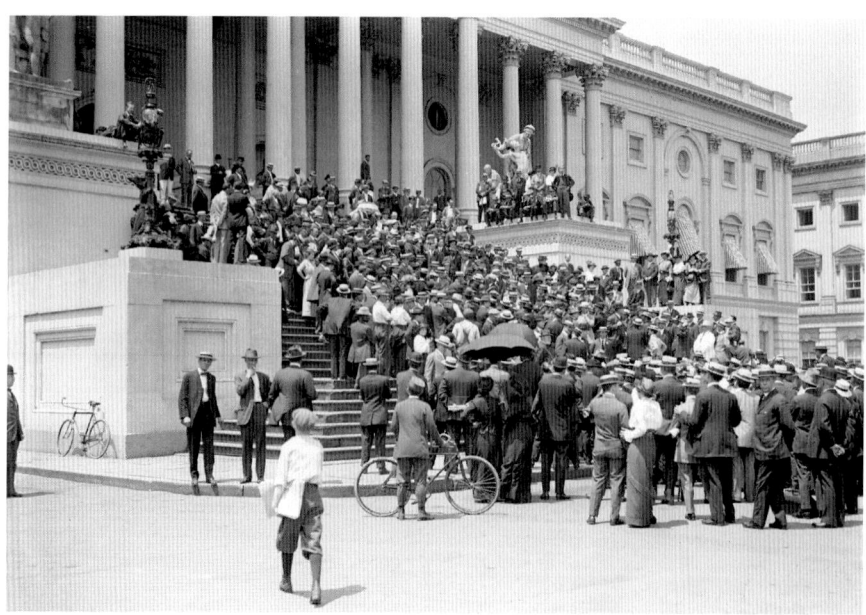

"General" Jacob Coxey speaks on the steps of the Capitol in 1894 at the apex of the first-ever March on Washington. Coxey and followers had walked there from Ohio, but the Montana contingent, being too far away to march, instead commandeered a train. *Library of Congress LC-DIG-hec-04236.*

Journalists thus painted Coxey's crusade in exaggerated images of warfare. The leader became known as "General Coxey" and his shambling men an "army." Sympathetic papers presented him as the hero of a "new French Revolution," while dissenters, noting his poverty-stricken followers, referred to it as a "campaign of squalor."

Thanks to advances in communications—both in popular media and within labor unions—such accounts stirred passions across the nation. "Coxeyites" sprang up in urban areas across the West, including San Francisco, Portland, Seattle, Tacoma, Spokane, and Butte. Through April of 1894, men vowed to join Coxey in Washington. But given the vast distances, they knew they had to travel by rail.

In Butte, passions simmered through several public demonstrations in April. Butte merchants, supportive of the city's unemployed yet tired of feeding them handouts, tried to persuade Northern Pacific to give them discounted passage. But railroads were among the hardest-hit companies of the recession, and indeed the recently bankrupted Northern Pacific argued that its management no longer had authority to grant such a favor.

Finally on April 24, at 2:00 a.m., the Coxeyites commandeered an old engine and six coal cars. Playing the John Wayne role was William Hogan, a wiry, Shakespeare-quoting, thirty-four-year-old teamster recently laid off from William A. Clark's Moulton mine. Hogan's men (including some knowledgeable railroad veterans) piled in and steamed up Homestake Pass. They nearly broke speed records on the ninety-mile trek to Bozeman, covering the final third at almost sixty miles an hour.

In Bozeman the men were greeted warmly. Townspeople gave them two tons of provisions, and they were able to trade their drafty coal cars for standard boxcars. But there they also learned of the slide at the Muir Tunnel, caused by torrential rains. Northern Pacific personnel had started to clear the mess, but when they learned that the next train expected through the tunnel was a stolen renegade, they hid their equipment and pulled out.

The Coxeyites, however, were men who wanted to work. Arriving at the slide, they found the cached shovels and waded into thick, slimy clay up to their knees. When they had nearly cleared the track, the top slid in again and they had to start over. For almost six hours they toiled, working in shifts because they had just fifteen shovels and two dull axes.

They knew they had to hurry. In Butte, assistant U.S. marshal M.J. Haley had struggled, in the labor-friendly city, to organize a posse, but he eventually rounded up eighty men, only fifteen of whom deserted before their train took off. By late afternoon, the Coxeyites were still working in three feet of mud but knew they were running out of time. Their engineer backed up the train to get a full head of steam, blew the whistle, rang the bell, and blasted through the obstruction. Minutes later, the Coxeyites arrived in Livingston, where locals donated another seventy-five dollars worth of provisions.

Why were locals so eager to help? In part, they wanted "Hogan's Army" to keep moving so that any confrontation would happen in the next town down the line. But at the same time, Coxey's populist cause had widespread support because it was tied to the Free Silver movement, which allied Montana's agricultural and mining interests against Eastern banks and manufacturers. Indeed, once the train was stolen, Northern Pacific division superintendent J.D. Finn had requested that Governor John Rickards call out the state militia, but Rickards refused.

If William Hogan is the populist hero in this legend, Finn is the corporate villain. In Butte, he'd tried to stop the Coxeyites through numerous legal maneuverings, had routed trains away from the city so they couldn't be commandeered, had pressured federal officials to assemble the ruffian mercenary "deputies," and now decided to sabotage his own railroad tracks. Near Greycliff, he ordered a cliff dynamited to spread more debris over the tracks. And for many miles to the east, he ordered that all trackside water tanks—used to replenish the steam engines—be emptied.

The Coxeyites easily removed the Greycliff slide and then paused to restore it so as to slow their more-indolent pursuers, joking that they wanted to leave the track in the condition they'd found it. But the lack of water proved more crippling. Between Greycliff and Columbus, the train had to slow to a crawl, with frequent stops for men to hurry down to the Yellowstone River to refill the tanks. For that purpose, they owned just a single bucket. Finally, as they neared a bridge over the river, a light appeared on the tracks behind them.

It was 1:00 a.m., twenty-three hours after they'd left Butte. The Coxeyites now faced a showdown with the law.

Hogan stopped the train in the middle of the bridge. The deputies, now numbering about sixty under Haley's command, approached. Now Hogan took his boldest move yet. He had several men walk out into the headlight of the pursuing locomotive, armed only with flags of the United States and the Butte Miners Union. They dared the deputies to shoot.

Haley had to back down. How could his posse shoot at unarmed men assembled under the flag? (At the time, the union was so powerful that its flag was nearly as symbolic as the Stars and Stripes.) The best he could do was to slowly follow his quarry and hope for another chance.

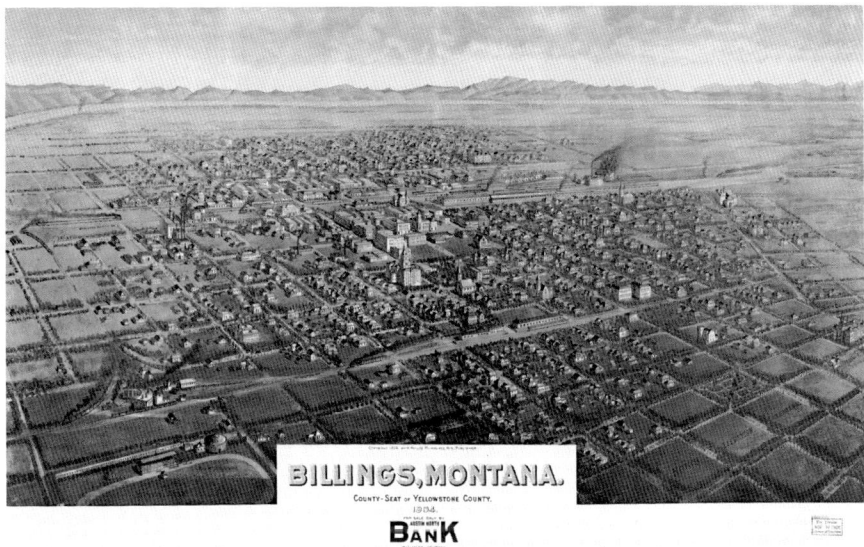

As Coxey's Army arrived in downtown Billings, shown here a few years later, a crowd of five hundred people offered them food—and fought the "deputies" who had been sent after them. *Library of Congress LC-DIG-pga-00223.*

    The Coxeyites creaked into Columbus, where they were again greeted by friendly crowds. William Cunningham, a Hogan deputy and former union president noted for his oratory, led an impromptu rally. Soon the deputies approached, guns drawn, but the Coxeyites jeered and cursed them as their train pulled away just before a riot could explode.

    At the next stop, in Billings, the fuse was shorter. Finn had wired Yellowstone County sheriff James Ramsey with orders to arrest Hogan's force. But Ramsey, apparently following the mood of the townspeople, decided it was not his quarrel. He told his deputies they should plan to be "out on business" when the train came through. And so his undersheriff wired back to Finn, tongue perhaps slightly in cheek, "All of [our] able bodied men are busy selling real estate. Stop Coxey's army at Livingston."

    So with little law enforcement present at the Billings depot, an "acting mayor" provided the Coxeyites with barrels of beef, bread, and potatoes. A crowd of nearly five hundred cheered, and as many as a hundred volunteered to join the expedition. Then, amid more oratory, Haley's pursuing deputies again approached, and this time their patience broke. They tried to fire on the engine, and in the general mêlée that followed, one of Haley's men fired into the crowd, fatally wounding a bystander.

The crowd turned on the deputies, disarming them and sending them scurrying for their lives back to their train. Some were beaten, and ten were arrested. As the shooting victim neared death, Billings sought revenge—not on the self-described "honest workingmen on a peaceful mission to Washington" but on the mob scraped together to pursue them in the name of the law.

Shaken, the Coxeyites continued eastward from Billings, still moving slowly with little available water. Hogan had led them through three escapes from the posse, but in truth he had not expected any of them. He'd hoped that Northern Pacific, like Montana law enforcement, would choose not to interfere with his train. Now that such hopes were dashed, he may have understood that the next outcome would not be so favorable.

In the aftermath of the violence in Billings, Northern Pacific officials and Governor Rickards convinced U.S. president Grover Cleveland to send out the regular army, the Twenty-second Infantry, based at Fort Keogh near Miles City. Finn provided a Northern Pacific train to take the troops westward to intercept the Coxeyites near Forsyth. Hogan's men, who respected the army where they had scorned the posse, immediately surrendered.

The anticlimax continued at the Capitol on May 1. Fewer than five hundred men had joined with Coxey at his final goal. And when they got there, police arrested Coxey for violating the "Keep Off the Grass" signs. He served thirty days, long enough for his army to disintegrate and the newspapers to find a new sensation.

For his leadership in stealing the train, Hogan served six months in prison; several of his assistants got thirty to sixty days. (William Cunningham, who now claimed to be not a Coxeyite at all but an undercover journalist for an Anaconda newspaper, got off.) The rest of the men were released and—to keep them occupied and off the local welfare rolls—were actually given materials and provisions to head to Washington via rafts on the Missouri River. As they left Fort Benton at the height of spring runoff, their scows spun crazily out of control. But the ragtag army made it all the way to St. Louis before having to face the fact that their cause was finished.

In the long run, however, Coxeyism proved not so much a failure as a crusade ahead of its time. In years since, we have come to adopt both its policies of federal work programs—a key response to the 1930s Great Depression—and its tactics of marching on Washington. Meanwhile, Montanans—specifically, the hardworking firebrands of industrial Butte—had played the most militant and colorful role in what the day's journalists labeled the most important series of national events since the Civil War. Less than five years into statehood, Montana had fully entered the national stage, and done so thanks to an urban army rather than a dusty frontier.

Montana Quarterly, 2008

Fame and Bandits

When the four bedraggled men rode into the mining boomtown of Red Lodge in late September of 1897, they were seeking fortune and everlasting fame. But the fortune quickly eluded them, and the path to fame—well, it is long and tortuous and rarely delivers the right people to the right destination.

Their planned fortune would come from robbing the Carbon County Bank. Three months previously, these same men had robbed a bank in Belle Fourche, South Dakota, and although that had not gone well—locals raised the alarm before the robbers got beyond the morning receipts, and they had to run with less than $100—they may have considered it on-the-job training.

They may have also been seeking revenge. Red Lodge banker John Chapman was an old Wyoming cattle baron, and in the previous twenty years of skirmishes among cattlemen, homesteaders, and rustlers, one of Chapman's major contributions had been organizing a posse that tracked down Butch Cassidy in 1893, leading to the outlaw's only stint in jail. But if this was the robbers' aim, they were poor planners: they targeted a bank across the street from Chapman's.

Their ambitions for fortune died when they dared not go through with the robbery. Apparently, upon arriving in town they approached marshal Byron St. Clair—whom they knew from his previous job in Fort Washakie, Wyoming—and suggested he go fishing. Legend has it that this was a bribe offering rather than a threat. But however he learned of their presence in town, St. Clair walked into the bank one morning to alert the cashier about the planned heist.

Soon Sheriff John Dunn organized a posse. Dunn was a small man with heavy, rounded shoulders and a thin, high-toned voice that he used infrequently. He was the kind of man who could stay in a saddle all day and who slept with one eye open—literally. A stitch in his eyelid prevented it from closing.

Dunn knew that Belle Fourche was offering rewards of $625 apiece for the capture of the desperadoes and that Oscar Stone, an attorney recently arrived in town from Detroit, had seen them escaping Red Lodge toward the northwest. Dunn's posse included Stone, Constable H.J. Calhoun of Columbus, and two Miles City–based stock inspectors, Dick Hicks and Billy Smith. They tracked the robbers north to Columbus and Lavina, gaining on them with every hour.

At this point, we're long overdue to meet these outlaws up close and personal. Unfortunately, however, bank robbers don't tend to keep meticulous diaries, so history has not left us a clear record of exactly who they were. One of them, we know, was Walt Putney, a longtime Wyomingite with a reputation as a horse thief. For now let's call the others X, Y, and Z.

At Columbus, Z allegedly left the group, perhaps taking an eastbound train, and escaped further pursuit. But his compatriots may not have even known they were being pursued. One report had them stopping for a drink at Jolley's Saloon in Lavina—and paying for it with a stolen Belle Fourche check. Late on Wednesday, September 22, they camped near an old cabin twenty-five miles north of Lavina, on the east slopes of the Little Snowy Mountains. The posse caught up to them as X was fastening his horse to a post about thirty yards from where he had unsaddled.

Dunn called for them to surrender. X jumped behind his horse and drew his gun, as Y and Putney dove behind a coulee. Gunfire from the posse injured X's wrist, causing him to drop his gun, and also toppled his horse. Dunn and Smith then advanced on the other two and got them to surrender, as X ran a mile on foot before being apprehended hiding behind a small outcropping.

After their arrest, the men gave a variety of names, including Charlie Frost, Tom Atkins, Frank Jones, and Thomas Jones, but in jail at Billings, two of them were identified by a teller at the Belle Fourche bank as the "Roberts brothers" who had robbed the bank. The posse split the reward money. Hicks used part of his share, in a gesture whose meaning has been lost to the ages, to buy hats for the prisoners. The outlaws were sent to South Dakota—where, on Halloween night, they escaped from jail.

That's why we don't know who X and Y were. In those days, there were few forms of ironclad identification: no driver's licenses, Social Security numbers, or fingerprints. We know about Putney only because he was immediately recaptured and his identity (though not an exact spelling of his name) established in his subsequent trial for the Belle Fourche robbery. (He was acquitted when his well-paid attorney located witnesses who would place Putney/Puteney/Punteney almost three hundred miles away on the day in question.) Without a trial, X and Y remained enigmas, the trails of their stolen horses leading west-southwest, toward the sunset.

ALTHOUGH WE MAY lament the difficulty of figuring out the facts regarding glamorous Old West criminal acts, it's little different than the situation today. Without the confirmation of a jury verdict, we can never know for sure who killed JonBenét Ramsey, Jimmy Hoffa, or Nicole Brown Simpson. But that uncertainty doesn't stop popular culture from advancing theories.

Within a few years of the Red Lodge incident, it became widely accepted that X was "Kid Curry" (real name: Harvey Logan), who with his brothers sometimes used the alias "Roberts." At five-foot-seven and 160 pounds, Curry was a small man with a large temper. Then about thirty years old, he had long devoured the dime novels that valorized the Robin Hood–style exploits of the outlaw Jesse James. This romanticism may have contributed to Curry going underground after killing a man in Landusky, Montana, in 1894. Curry claimed it was self-defense but worried that he wouldn't get a fair trial in a town named after his victim, Pike Landusky. Curry relocated to Wyoming's Hole in the Wall country, on the southeast slopes of the Bighorn Mountains, where he eventually became a leader of a rather nasty gang of criminals.

Another gang kingpin was George "Flat Nose" Currie, whose ugly mug centered on a nose that could belong to a failed boxer. The Pinkertons—a national private-detective agency that ranked and pursued outlaws much like the FBI does today—identified Flat Nose as Wyoming's "king of the rustlers." He was credited with leading the Belle Fourche and several other robberies before being killed by authorities in April of 1900. He is now assumed to be Z: a planner of the Red Lodge robbery who left his compatriots after they failed to execute it.

Today, most people associate these outlaws—one group called the Hole in the Wall Gang, and an associated one called the Wild Bunch—with Butch Cassidy (real name: Robert Leroy Parker). That's probably because Cassidy

OUTLAWS

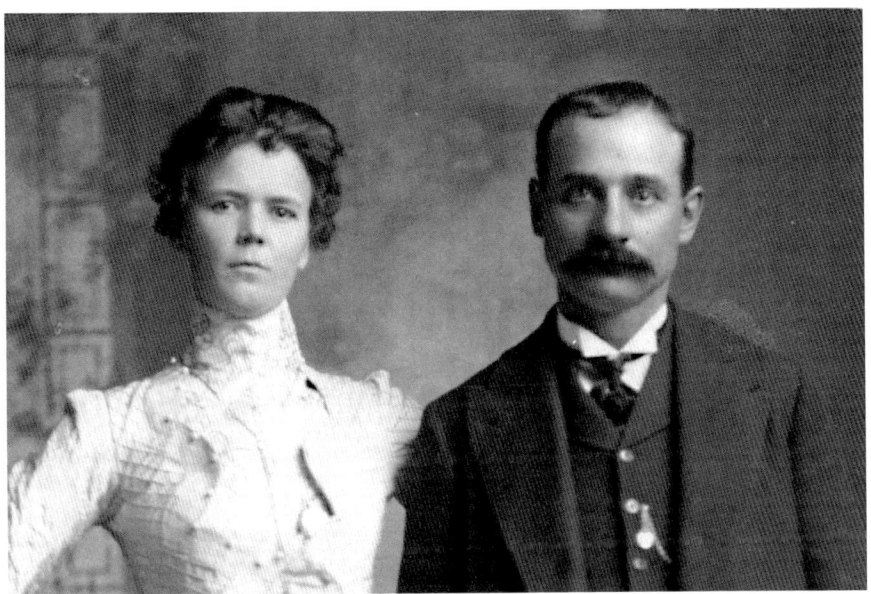

Pinkerton's National Detective Agency included this photo, labeled Harvey Logan, in its "Wild Bunch" folder. Logan, also known as Kid Curry, was hungry for the fame of banditry but learned the wrong lessons about how to achieve it. *Library of Congress LC-DIG-ppmsca-07624.*

was the most likeable of this gruesome crew, with his piercing eyes and rapid-fire talk, his loyalty toward fellow thieves and honor toward pursuers. Cassidy avoided violence and once declined to kill a Pinkerton agent who was ready to unmask his alias. But Cassidy was not involved in the Belle Fourche or Red Lodge escapades, and some historians believe his role in the gangs has been exaggerated.

Speaking of exaggeration, meet Butch's friend Harry Longabaugh, nicknamed the Sundance Kid because he was once jailed in the Wyoming town of that name. Speculation now has Sundance as Y; the thin evidence includes the fact that he had once worked in Lavina and so would have been familiar with that country. Sundance attracted little attention in those years; indeed it was hard for observers to even agree what he looked like. (He was anywhere from five-foot-seven to six feet tall; weighed 165 or 190 pounds; had light, light brown, or black hair; and had blue, gray, black, or brown eyes.) It was only later—when he and Butch, the last of the Wild Bunch still alive and uncaptured, fled to Argentina—that he became a celebrity. After that, he was retroactively inserted into situations where he may not have been present and given qualities such as a fast draw that may have more appropriately belonged to the other Kid—Curry.

That's ironic, because it was Curry, the worshiper of Jesse James legends, who had the strongest ambitions for fame. He did meet with a few years of mild notoriety after 1898, successfully robbing banks and trains. Curry apparently basked in published descriptions of himself as "the Napoleon of crime" or "the executioner of the Wild Bunch" and in accounts saying that "no prison has been strong enough hold him" or that the Union Pacific Railroad spent $500,000 to capture him. (Such accounts were almost certainly exaggerated, but like the exaggerations of today's reality television, they were ones that pleased everybody: Curry got notoriety, the Pinkertons got bigger budgets, media outlets boosted sales, and the public was entertained.)

Two factors tarnished Curry's fame, at least one of which was his own fault. He apparently learned the wrong lesson from his dime novels and focused on the violence rather than the Robin Hood compassion. Unlike James or Cassidy, Curry killed multiple respected lawmen—sometimes when they were unaware or unarmed—and mistreated innocent victims in his robberies. And what's worse for an aspiring legend, his death was unclear and ignoble.

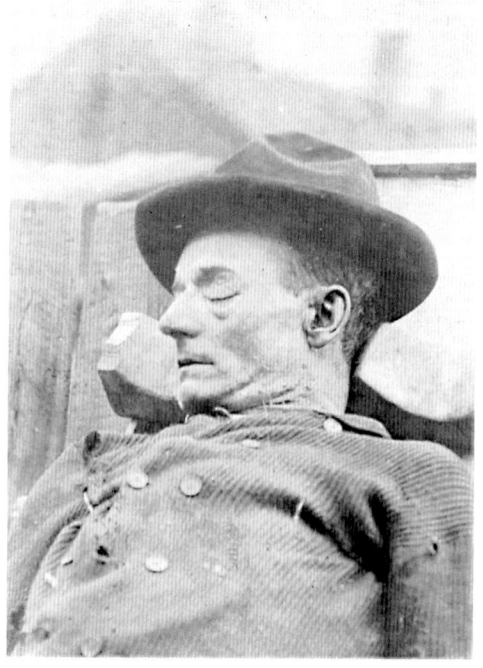

In a 1904 shootout following an unsuccessful train robbery near Parachute, Colorado, an outlaw was wounded. As his compatriots fled, he briefly held off the posse and then shot himself in the head. Authorities later identified the body as Curry and collected a reward. Among the doubts that soon surfaced was the fact that this man lacked a wrist scar from the Lavina shooting. The doubts

The Pinkertons claimed that this man, who killed himself near Parachute, Colorado, after a 1904 train robbery, was Kid Curry. The ignoble end thwarted his dreams of fame. *Library of Congress LC-DIG-ppmsca-07625.*

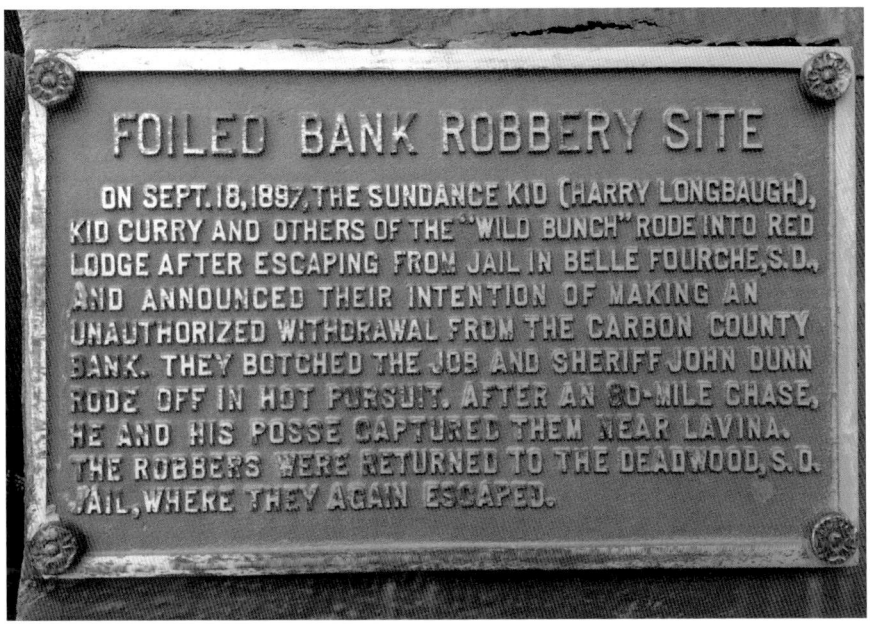

This plaque in downtown Red Lodge was erected about the time of the movie *Butch Cassidy and the Sundance Kid*. By elevating Sundance above "Kid Curry," it thus honors our memories of 1960s outlaw images more than the thieves' own dreams of fame. *Courtesy Kari Clayton.*

increased when Curry was allegedly spotted in South America…but then he basically vanished.

Had Kid Curry committed suicide rather than drawing his final shootout to an epic conclusion? Or, if that man was not Curry, had the Kid gone straight and hidden his past, or died quietly, drunk and alone? None of these are the way we think bold, legendary bandits should go.

Indeed, Kid Curry's romanticism lives on in many of us, in the ways we seek connections to these outrageous acts of yore. For example, on the site of the Carbon County Bank, a building—not constructed until two years after the incident—boasts a plaque citing this "foiled bank robbery site" where the Sundance Kid (who gets top billing) and Kid Curry (no mention of Putney) "botched" their attempt. In a sense, the plaque—unofficial and slightly erroneous—honors 1969 as much as 1897. That's when the silver screen brought us Paul Newman as Butch and Robert Redford as Sundance, acting out an indelible, though twisted, version of Kid Curry's dreams for everlasting fame.

Montana Quarterly, 2010

The Trials of John L. Smith

On Monday, February 22, 1926, John L. "Red-Eye" Smith got off a little bay pony outside the Billings police station, walked in, and said, "I guess you can take me."

The officers responded with surprise and amusement.

"You can lock me up. I give myself up."

"What for?"

"I've just shot a n——."

Smith was known to police. A trapper and hunter, he'd come to Montana almost fifty years earlier. He served as a deputy sheriff in the late 1880s and early 1890s. He was a man of nerve, old-timers said. In the late 1890s, he shot a man in a quarrel; he was not prosecuted. Since then he had led a nomadic existence, visiting Billings when he was not out in the mountains. He was now seventy-three years old and staying in the back room of a shack on the south side of town owned by his friend John Burckle.

The victim, Alfred Black Bird, was actually half African American and half Crow. His father had been a buffalo soldier with the Twenty-fifth Infantry, stationed at Fort Custer in the early 1890s. Alfred was thirty-six years old and married, with a two-year-old daughter. When police arrived at the scene, they found him lying facedown. His wife and his foster mother were chanting a Crow death song over his body. His daughter was sobbing from fright.

History does not record the tone with which Smith made his bold statement to police. Could it have been irony? While records are unclear, it's likely that no white man had ever been convicted of murdering a black man in Montana. Smith probably didn't believe he'd be the first.

Black Bird's troubles had begun the previous week. He had come to Billings with his family from his allotment in the Bighorn district after receiving his annuity money. Then he lost more than $100. Black Bird filed a police report saying the money had been stolen, but he later implied that he might have left it in a pocket when he traded shirts with a man named Pretty Coyote, who had by then left for Edgar, a small town about thirty miles to the southwest. Apparently believing that Smith was still a lawman, Black Bird asked Smith to accompany him to Edgar.

Smith was well suited to such a job. He spoke Crow. He had lived for many years in Silesia, not far from Edgar, where he had been married to a Crow woman. (Among his numerous nicknames was "Squaw" Smith.) To do the job, Smith asked Black Bird for ten dollars; later, he asked Black Bird's wife for another fifteen.

Black Bird, Smith, and two others made the trip to Edgar on Friday. When they demanded the money, Pretty Coyote told them he had already sent it back to Billings and that Black Bird should get it soon. Somehow he managed to convince the men that he was telling the truth, and they left empty-handed.

By Monday, Black Bird had apparently received the money, and he started thinking about the twenty-five dollars he paid Smith. At about 10:30 a.m., he went to see if he could get some of it back. Smith and Black Bird, walking together, quarreled as they approached the shack where Smith was living. According to a neighbor, J.M. Bess, Smith invited Black Bird in, indicating that he would give him the money. Then Smith pulled a gun from under his pillow and shot him in the chest. Black Bird staggered ten or twelve steps and then fell over dead.

Though it was Smith's first time in a courtroom on such a serious charge, it was hardly his first public trial. Almost twenty years earlier, when Smith was living in Cody, Wyoming, and hauling logs to the site of a government dam across the Stinkingwater River, an incident he was involved in made headlines back East.

"Cody's Bad Man Runs to Escape a Few Stones," read the headline on a story by Caroline Lockhart. It described Smith as "somewhere near six feet tall, with a rather formidable breadth and thickness of shoulder, and like the South American animal whose ugliness is its defense, Smith's best protection is his face, though he habitually packs a gun in a holster under his arm."

The man she portrayed was mean, bored, and racist. "Guess I'll have to drive over a few of them dagoes," she reported Smith as saying as he harnessed his four-horse team one morning. "I'm one of the most notorious dago wranglers that ever jumped up, and I can wrangle railroad hoboes to a fare-ye-well. I'll do any old thing. I'm a game one. I'm a killer—me, Smith!"

Italian workman Luigi Ammendolea was swinging his pick and reminiscing about the pomegranates and cathedrals of Rome when suddenly "Squaw Smith came around the curve and bestowed upon him a title which was a long way from being his name." Ammendolea, despite being under five feet tall and "as plump as a herring," picked up some rocks and started throwing them at Smith. "The Bad Man sat on his logs, too dazed as yet to move by the unexpected display of hostilities. He had bullied his way for so long and called himself a Bad Man so frequently that he had got himself in a frame of mind wherein he really believed that he was what he would like to be." Smith was saved only by the noon whistle calling Ammendolea to dinner.

Lockhart later expanded the article into a novel, centered on a bad man who drifts onto a Wyoming ranch and schemes to take it over. "His shoulders were thick and broad…His jaw was square, but it evidenced brutality rather than determination." She named him Smith, and in a line that would become a refrain, she closed the first chapter, "'I'm a killer, me—Smith,' he said, and grinned."

The fictional Smith appears far worse than any one real man could be. In the opening chapter alone, he steals a dude's horse and then kills an Indian for his blanket. Later he rustles cattle, fondly recalls the married woman he seduced and abandoned, and deliberately shoots a woman who has just saved his life and then tries to swindle her.

A bestseller in 1911, *Me-Smith* was favorably reviewed, and serialized in the *New York World*. Years later, cowboy actor William S. Hart wrote to Lockhart, "I consider your *Me Smith* one of the greatest characters ever drawn." Such notoriety must have reached even Smith in one of his haunts in the country between Billings and Cody. His reaction? According to Lockhart, he loved the publicity: he told her he should get half the proceeds from the book since it was, after all, about him.

During the Black Bird trial, Smith's attorneys were Roy Allan and Kenneth Simmons, "newly minted lawyers who had never before been within a mile of a murder case," Allan's son Richmond later recalled. They had "no illusions about Smith's culpability, [but] got a kick out of defending him" because of his colorful character and ties to the fading frontier. In later years, Allan would frequently reminisce about Smith, a crack shot who told magnificent stories about the old trapper John "Liver-Eating" Johnston.

Their defense did not exactly deny Smith's misdeeds. They argued that Black Bird was drunk during the trip to Edgar and, especially, during the Monday morning quarrel. They said the quarrel was over a gun sight that Smith had refused to make. They also pointed out that while Smith was seventy-three years old, Black Bird was young, six feet tall, and 190 pounds. They said Black Bird carried a stick and a rock. Afraid of the man, Smith went inside Burckle's cabin and fastened the catch on the door. But Black Bird kept coming. Smith fired in self-defense.

Three women testified for the prosecution. They said that Black Bird was not drunk. They said Burckle had told Black Bird not to go near Smith, as he would get shot. The neighbor, J.M. Bess, also testified, saying that Black Bird was not carrying anything when he approached the shack. He was not threatening. He said Smith had stood over Black Bird's body and said that no n—— was going to kick in his door and get away with it. Black Bird's foster mother said Burckle had planted the stick and rock on Black Bird while Smith was confessing at the police station.

All five of the key prosecution witnesses were Indian or black.

Smith's attorneys called character witnesses, including a doctor and two judges, one of whom had known Smith "since the memory of man runneth not to the contrary." When asked about his previous shooting scrapes, they countered that none had happened in Yellowstone County.

The jury deliberated for twenty-three hours. They asked to see the Burckle premises, and so the judge sent them on a tour. Nevertheless, the jurors sent him a note saying they hopelessly disagreed. The judge told them to try again. During a recess, a reporter noted that Smith "has apparently borne the strain of the trial well," talking with friends, usually of matters other than the trial.

Finally, the jury came back with a verdict—not guilty. Smith was free to go. He disappeared into history: his obituary was not recorded in Billings, Cody, or any place in between. But it seems almost certain that he died freer and happier than Alfred Black Bird.

Tellingly, however, the defense had investigated yet another strategy to prove Smith's innocence. It would have been unusual, and—given that it showed the hallmarks of Smith's considerable self-regard—it might well have backfired. Smith's attorneys wired Caroline Lockhart to ask if she would serve as a character witness for the real-life protagonist of her acclaimed novel: "JOHN L RED EYE ME SMITH FACING TRIAL HERE FOR THE MURDER OF A BREED INDIAN NAMED ALFRED BLACKBIRD KILLING COMMITTED IN SELF DEFENSE BY SMITH SMITH WITHOUT FUNDS WE ARE HIS ATTORNEYS WILL YOU HELP HIM CAN YOU COME TO BILLINGS WIRE IMMEDIATELY SIMMONS AND ALLAN LAWYERS."

Lockhart's response gives us faith that fiction, at least in this case, may have a better understanding of justice than the law. "He murdered the Indian in cold blood," she later told a reporter. "I wouldn't help him. He was a killer."

Montana: The Magazine of Western History, 2004

Part III

Economies

Camp Senia and Montana's Dude Ranching Heritage

A 2008 wildfire west of Red Lodge made statewide headlines when it briefly threatened structures at Red Lodge Mountain ski resort. But the fire's historical damage came on its first day, when it engulfed five summer cabins on the West Fork of Rock Creek. Two of the cabins had originally been constructed as part of a place called Camp Senia—a fascinating link to Montana's dude ranching past.

Dude ranches often get short shrift in Montana history. We're apt to dismiss them as "fake" ranches, and their patrons as, well, dudes. But in its 1920s heyday, dude ranching transformed the state's economy, culture, and self-image.

After World War I, cattle prices crashed. Drought plagued the plains. Demand for copper fell, slowing mining in Butte (and in Red Lodge, which mined coal that fired industry). For the first time in Montana's history, the economic promise of the frontier was evaporating. No matter how hard you worked to try to take advantage of Montana's natural resources, markets wouldn't reward you.

But "the frontier" had always had two faces—economic and romantic—and in the 1920s, the romantic promise still beckoned. In the industrialized East, people spent most of their time in factories or offices, surrounded by pollution and crowds. Many were still new to urban life and found it constricted, formal, pointless, dirty, and/or mean. Many of those who could afford vacations often went to stuffy seaside resorts, where high-society traditions kept a firm rein on their activities, their enthusiasms, and even their attire. Others went to Europe, but their getaway spots had been devastated by war.

So imagine those folks receiving a brochure that seemed to understand their "longing for jagged skylines, tumultuous streams, glorious hours of physical exertion, [and] the everlasting presence of the mountains." The brochure suggests a visit to a dude ranch, a place called Camp Senia. Afterward, it says, "you will be a freer, surer, more interesting person. You'll even like yourself better after a Rocky Mountain vacation."

At the dude ranch, your host would be a combination of today's fishing guide, bed-and-breakfast operator, restaurateur, and horse whisperer. The dude ranchers introduced local traditions to newcomers who wanted to live a rugged outdoor life but needed a mentor to teach them how to cope with the terrain. In this sense they resembled nearly all Anglo-Saxons who have ever arrived in Montana, such as, for example, Teddy Roosevelt, Owen Wister, and Frederic Remington, all of them classic dudes in that they arrived with more gear than sense, eager to see and learn and then return home.

The profession of dude ranching arose organically from dozens of folks across the region making individual decisions. Two of them were Al Croonquist and Senia Pollari of Red Lodge. When they married in 1914, they probably didn't set out to capitalize on societal trends. They just knew that they liked to fish and explore the mountains. They spent three years looking for a site to build a fishing camp, finally choosing a spot twelve miles up the West Fork from Red Lodge. Their site hugged the burbling stream in a grove of lodgepole pine that had been spared from a devastating wildfire twenty years previously.

Construction was delayed during World War I, when Al had to run his family's mercantile while his brother served in Europe, but resumed in 1919 just in time to catch the growing wave of dudes. Throughout the 1920s, the Croonquists kept adding on to their compound and boosting their marketing efforts in Chicago, Minneapolis, and Boston.

The Camp Senia letterhead featured Al's line drawing of snowcapped peaks, spruce trees, streams, and people on horseback, with an inset depicting a man wearing a bandana and a cowboy hat. In text under that letterhead, Al would boast that life at the camp was "like its environment—rough, rugged, friendly, scrupulously clean, wholesome, and of a nature that will pull you back again." A visit was not merely a stopover; many guests stayed a month, and some stayed the entire summer. And after they returned home, as if from a rejuvenating spa, "the wind-and-sun tan may fade. But you'll still be a different person after a real adventure in the Rockies—different for life!"

Croonquist was appealing to nostalgia for rural life and also to an audience captivated by newly popular Western movies and novels. The country was awash in romantic images of honorable cowboys playing out grand conflicts on a now-closed frontier. But that closing made a no-longer-frontier vacation

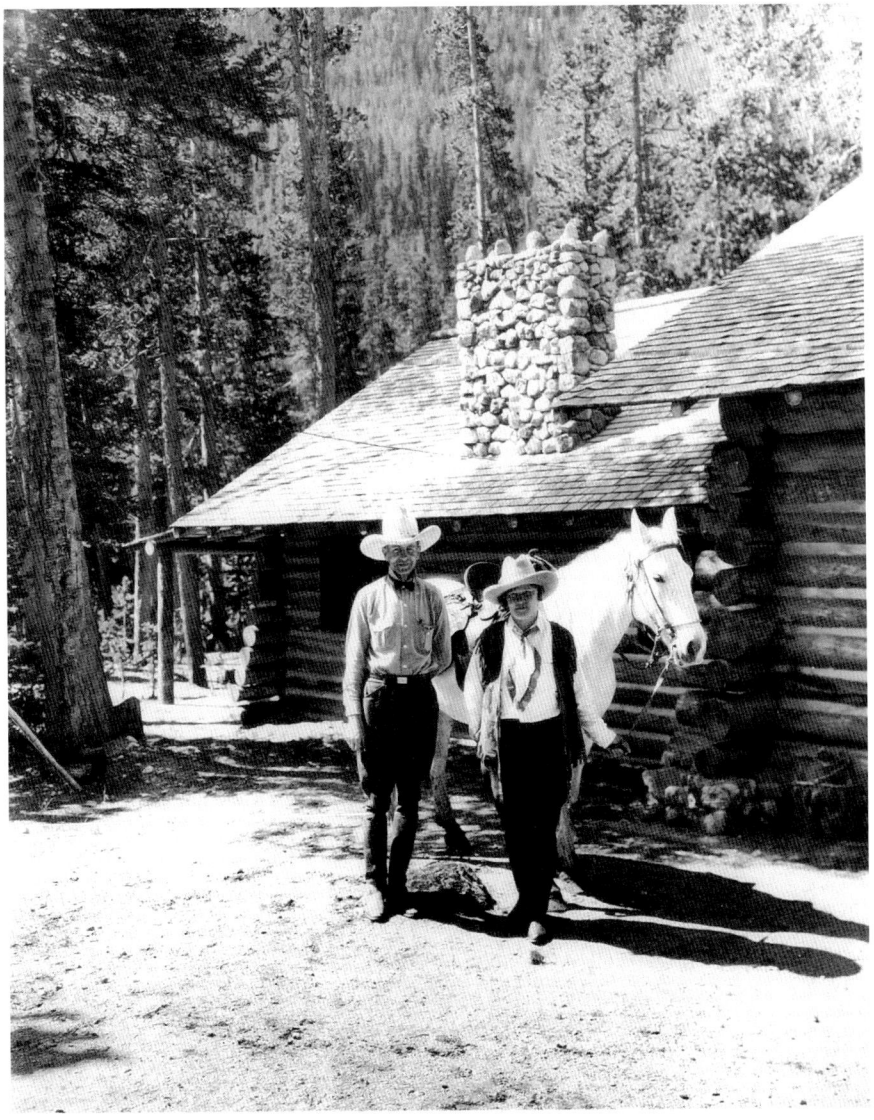

Al and Senia (Pollari) Croonquist built the first dude ranch in the Beartooths starting in 1917. Camp Senia was located in a lodgepole pine forest twelve miles west of Red Lodge. The log and stone architecture and stylized cowboy attire appealed to Easterners who wanted a frontier vacation. *Courtesy Senia Hart family.*

safe for popular consumption. Camp Senia, a brochure claimed, would bring you "the lore of the old picturesque West, of the days when mountaineering was known only to the hardy pioneer and the Indian."

When we look back at dude ranching life, it's easy to quote from marketing materials because they still exist in archives. But oral traditions suggest that marketing was a very small portion of Camp Senia's success. Most of it was hard work. Senia Pollari Croonquist and her Finnish-immigrant sisters anchored the domestic staff, up at 5:00 a.m. to work on breakfast that featured eggs, milk, vegetables, and meat brought up daily from the family ranch. A series of cooks, notoriously ill-tempered, quit midseason, and the family kept having to fill in until Al could go into town and hire a new one. (The camp's difficulties retaining kitchen help were so well known in Red Lodge that the first local production at a fancy new theater called the Theatorium was "a musical love story of Camp Senia" titled "Wanted: A Cook.")

This dichotomy between the marketing that Easterners saw and the work that Westerners performed may help explain the mixed feelings about dude ranches that endure to this day. The dude ranch often epitomized class struggle: run by extroverted, well-bred Easterners, who made a living more from connections to capital than from outdoor skills. (In this, the Croonquists were an exception.) The land became valuable not for its agricultural production potential, but for its scenery—and sometimes for the package of services designed to help people consume that scenery in luxury. This meant that while "real" ranchers demonstrated their mastery by producing physical products such as beef, dude ranchers could be seen as kowtowing to wealthy but ignorant customers.

But this sort of armchair class analysis is a luxury of our times. In the 1920s, Al and Senia Croonquist simply wanted to find a way to make a living in Montana. Economic development boiled down to exporting products or importing people. And the Croonquists liked people, were good with people, and enjoyed sharing their passions with people.

One of those passions was fishing. Al and his staff stocked dozens of area streams and lakes with fish. They would load up ten-gallon milk cans with three-inch fingerling trout (one thousand to a can) and pack them on horses to remote lakes. At many of these lakes, now in the Absaroka-Beartooth Wilderness, the chance to catch a trout at the end of an arduous multi-day journey remains a highlight of a Western vacation.

It was thus the dude ranchers who introduced Montana to the economic incentives of conservation. Their dudes wanted more fish, wildlife, and public lands. They saw the environment as something to appreciate rather than subdue. They saw the frontier as an adventure and spiritual quest rather than a historical phase. The political ramifications of these shifts are still playing out today.

Dude ranchers also played a role in emerging ideas of Western culture. For example, at Camp Senia, the men who built the cabins always left the logs rounded. Traditional Finn architecture of the time squared off logs for a home; rounded logs were deemed suitable only for barns and outbuildings. But dudes preferred the rounded look. That architecture, which arose at dude ranches across the region, soon came to be known as the Western Rustic style. Ironically, its popularity came as much from Easterners' hunger for "simple" country life as from the tastes or needs of the cabin-builders themselves.

But Western Rustic emphasized the relaxed nature of everyday life at a dude ranch. As another Camp Senia brochure proclaimed, "There is no fuss of formalities up here. Folks who have been out before bring their own western togs with them. If you have none, we suggest you buy them when you get here, and hang your city clothes on the hitching post until you leave."

Camp Senia had not been the first dude ranch in the state (the OTO near Gardiner dates back to the turn of the century). Nor was it terribly prominent. Al Croonquist did co-found the national Dude Ranchers Association in 1926 and served as its first vice-president. But after the stock market crash of 1929, Camp Senia guests canceled their reservations for the following season, and banks called in their loans. After a few failed attempts at restructuring, in the late 1930s the buildings became individual summer residences under a Forest Service lease.

Yet, in part because of their solid design and construction, the log and stone cabins retained much of their character and structural soundness. So did the community that inhabited them. Many of the cabin owners had ties to the old dude ranch, and Forest Service regulations (plus, since 1988, inclusion on the National Register of Historic Places) kept renovations to a minimum.

In the last few years, the Forest Service and cabin owners had been preparing for wildfire. Projects throughout the area sought to reduce hazardous fuels, and cabin owners cleared defensible space around their structures. But in November 2007, a windstorm blew down twenty thousand acres of trees across the Beartooth Ranger District, including thousands of trees up the West Fork.

The Forest Service cleared the road and fallen trees in the camp. Camp Senia residents then spent much of the early summer clearing around their

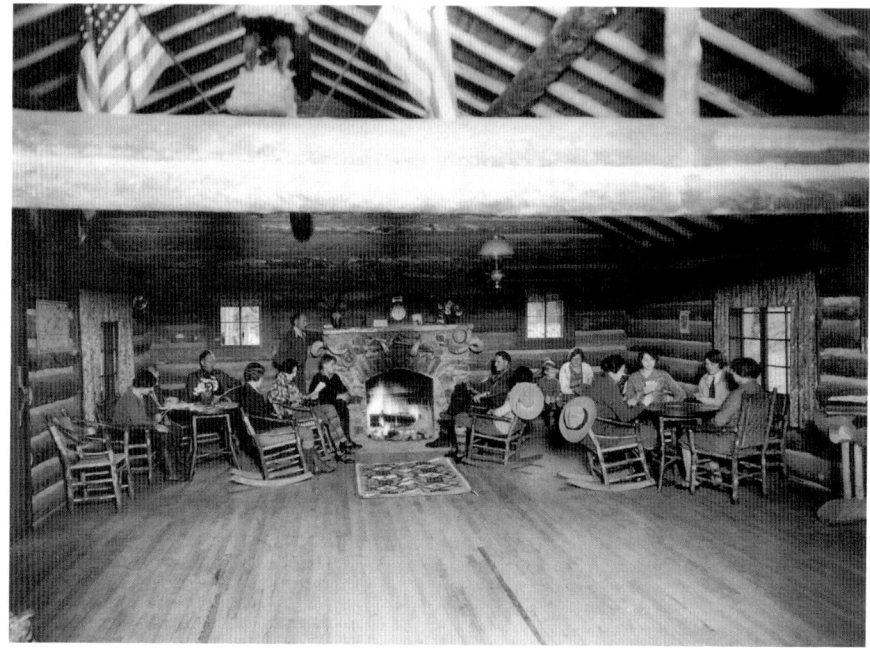

In the main lodge at Camp Senia, guests of the 1920s would gather to read or play cards. The use of rounded, rather than hewn, logs to construct the cabin was part of the emerging Western Rustic style favored by dudes. *Courtesy Senia Hart family.*

cabins. Because of that defensible space, firefighters—who arrived soon after the fire blew up, thanks to fast action by area fire departments and the Forest Service—faced less risk when trying to save cabins. Less risk meant less destruction.

And so Camp Senia will live on. The area is blackened, the ecosystem adjusting. The community has changed, too, since the camp's heyday: it is no longer vacationing Easterners but summer residents, many with ties to Billings and Red Lodge. Despite these differences, however, what lives on is a vision of the good life in Montana.

When the Croonquists urged guests to "hang your city clothes on the hitching post," they were pushing an informality that continues to be a hallmark of life here for visitors and residents alike. Until the 1920s, Montana had been a place where you might homestead a hardscrabble ranch or swing a pick in a mine—where most people were braving the cold weather so as to work hard and make a living.

But as moneymaking opportunities receded, it was dude ranchers who showed Montana a new self-image. At Camp Senia, as in many parts of the state, Montanans brave the cold for non-economic reasons: the open, friendly attitude; the spiritual connection to nature and wildlife; and the rejuvenation offered by spending as much time as possible in the glorious outdoors.

Montana Quarterly, 2008

ORIGINS OF THE BEARTOOTH HIGHWAY

On a winter evening in 1924, seven men met at a Red Lodge hotel. Aware that one of their town's two coal mines was closing and the other was scaling back production, the men talked about what the community should do.

Red Lodge had been booming: in the 1910s, it had typically produced more than a million tons of coal per year. But more recently, it had been wracked by strikes and cursed by geology. Its underground veins of coal could never be mined as cheaply as the recently discovered surface veins near Colstrip. The combination suggested a dire future; Montana was already littered with examples of what happened to a town when its mines closed.

During the meeting, six of the men—Red Lodge mayor Carl Koehn, hotelier Tom Pollard, newspaper publisher Oliver H.P. Shelley, James Plunkett, Dominick Marino, and William Pinkney—apparently mostly listened. The seventh man, Dr. Johann Carl Frederick Siegfriedt (1879–1940), made a bold, even crazy proposal: Red Lodge could be saved by building a road through nowhere.

Who was Siegfriedt, and why was he at this meeting? He had landed in nearby Bearcreek in 1906, just one year after the railroad arrived there, as Bearcreek's own coal mines amped up production. He was a six-foot-tall, large-framed man who loved fishing and hunting in the surrounding mountains. He was bald. He was devoted to his wife, Lilly, who was frequently described as being in "delicate health." They had no children, and his relatives rarely visited. But Siegfriedt found a wider family in the community he served.

He spent a great deal of time with those townsfolk. As the official doctor of one of the Bearcreek mines, he received a salary deducted from each miner's paycheck—and had to respond to every mine emergency. (He always prescribed injured miners a stiff drink of good bourbon. Management soon made it available in the mine's emergency room, and miners learned to have some even before the good doctor arrived.) In the rough-and-tumble town, he also responded to other emergencies, once successfully sewing together a knifing victim atop a tavern pool table.

Siegfriedt even ate with his patients. The dining room at the Washoe Boarding House had a long table where miners ate communally and a smaller table for the upper class, such as ministers, the school principal, and the mine surveyor. The doctor preferred eating at the long table, where he was known as a stunning conversationalist with an "infectious cheerfulness."

"He was sometimes, some say always, lax in sending bills to his patients," recalled Thomas Lewis in *Red Lodge: Saga of a Western Area*. His primary goal was treating patients; if they later paid him for that treatment, fine. Friends recalled badgering him to tell what they owed, finally getting a reluctant, "OK, give me five dollars."

He was known to all as "Doc." He never used any of his three first names—before becoming a doctor, he was known as "Sig" or "Siggy"—and most people didn't learn what the J.C.F. stood for until his obituary. He did not patronize any of Bearcreek's many bars, nor its churches. Though he had been quite a musician in his Iowa youth, and put himself through college in part by playing the zither, he did not play music publicly. Relaxation came primarily in the form of bridge games with close friends.

His other passion was public involvement. He was the sort of person who would join every club he could find. He served five terms as mayor of Bearcreek, his only election loss coming when he forgot to file the appropriate paperwork and the defeated candidate had him retroactively disqualified. (After moving to Red Lodge in 1930, he ran for mayor on a platform acknowledging that although gambling and prostitution were illegal, they were also mainstays of the local economy and culture. His planks thus included "bring in twenty more slot machines" and "start some new houses of pleasure." He won easily.)

One year, during a strike at the Bearcreek mines, the mayor made a practical suggestion. Using the striking miners as volunteer labor, they could cover Main Street with scoria rock waste from the mines. This inexpensive

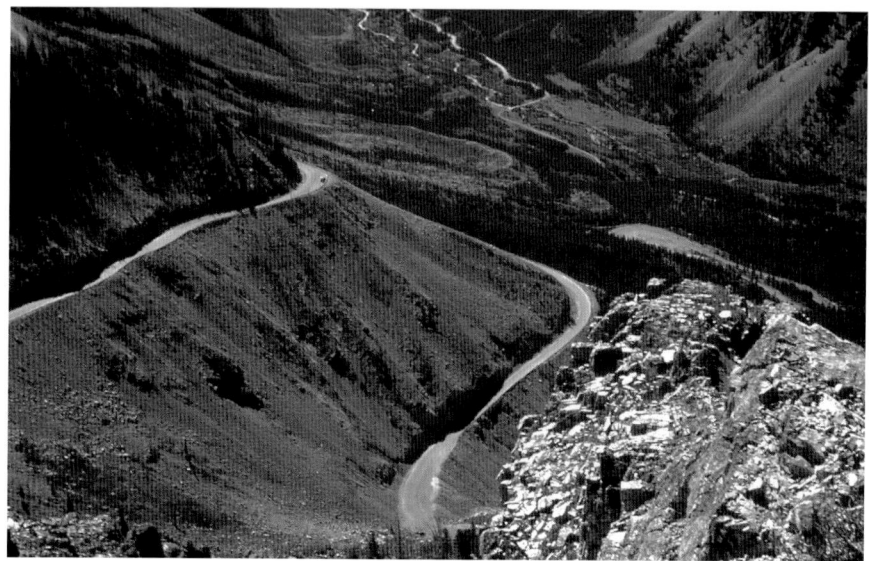

The Beartooth Highway, shown here switchbacking up the plateau south of Red Lodge, is an engineering marvel dating from the early 1930s. *National Park Service photo.*

solution proved a great improvement on the previous dust and mud, and aligned with Siegfriedt's interest in road construction.

Automobiles were still new at the time. Most people traveled by train. Recreational long-distance auto travel was a specialty hobby of a certain class of people who often gathered together in clubs (much like downhill skiers would in the 1940s and '50s). Cross-state routes had not yet been organized by number ("Route 12") and were instead known by name ("The Yellowstone Trail") or colorful logo.

In the early 1910s, Siegfriedt had become president of an association called the Black and White Trail. Early on, it apparently planned to improve the route to Cody, Wyoming, largely following the path of an old wagon road called the Meeteetse Trail. Everything was put on hold during World War I, when Siegfriedt entered the medical corps and did research at Yale. And by 1919, Siegfriedt had a better idea for the Black and White Trail: it should go over the Beartooths to Cooke City.

He was hardly the first person to make such a proposal. In 1882, General Philip Sheridan left Yellowstone Park via Cooke City with a party of more than 120 people. His planned route blocked by a forest fire, he instead crossed the Beartooths. Since then, many people had suggested a road or railroad along Sheridan's route to the lucrative Cooke City mines. But Siegfriedt actually did something about it.

In 1919, Siegfriedt directed the construction of thirteen switchbacks up the northeast side of Mount Maurice, south of Bearcreek, using striking miners for labor. Horses and dynamite were supposedly paid for by subscribers to the Black and White Trail club, although given Siegfriedt's lax bookkeeping standards, the money probably came mostly from his own pocket. During a 1922 strike, they continued the work and sent a party to survey the full length of the route.

The project proved too big for volunteer laborers and a doctor's spare change. But when Red Lodge faced its crisis two years later, Siegfriedt saw his opportunity and scaled up his ambitions. He told the men that they should insist on a road to Cooke City—starting from Red Lodge instead of Bearcreek if they preferred—and that they should get the federal government to pay for it.

TODAY WE KNOW the stunning results of that meeting. The road commonly known as the Beartooth Highway (though it had no official name until 2002, when it became the Beartooth All-American Road) is one of the few places in the entire country where you can drive for miles at a time above treeline in alpine tundra, with views of craggy peaks, lakes, and endless plains off to each side. Peripatetic television newsman Charles Kuralt once called it the most scenic highway in America.

The road's gravity-defying splendor attracts tourists from throughout the region and the world. Some are content to drive the road in awe, while others, from spring skiers to backpackers, use it to access the peaks of the Beartooth and Absaroka ranges. These visitors have indeed replaced mining as an economic engine in both Red Lodge and Cooke City—to a comprehensive degree not fully appreciated until 2005.

On May 20 of that year, after a nine-inch rainfall, a series of mudslides swept away several sections of the switchbacking highway just a week before its scheduled opening for the summer. Repairs were estimated at $15 to $20 million, and political leaders worked with remarkable speed to find the budget in time to start repairs during the short summer season. Crews worked twenty-four hours a day, six days a week, to finish repairs by October so that the road could reopen the following summer. Siegfriedt's dream had become a treasure valued by the nation as a whole.

Thus, from today's perspective, it's hard to appreciate how creative, and how foolish, Siegfriedt's idea was at the time. The creativity came from grasping the growing importance of automotive transportation, at a time when one could make the sixty-mile drive from Red Lodge to Billings in less than three hours. Roads could be cheaper than railways to build, and they could cover steeper slopes. And roads didn't require dependence on a well-capitalized railroad company.

The foolishness came from the notion that a community could simply request a road covering more than sixty miles of rugged, steep terrain at elevations topping ten thousand feet, and somehow it would materialize. Standard federal policy was to fund only half the costs of any new road construction, with the other half coming locally. Red Lodge boosters might argue that since this road would go entirely through an unpopulated national forest, there were no local entities to put up their share—but that still could set a dangerous precedent.

"That it was a seemingly hopeless attempt from the start was apparent to everyone but the men who started it," wrote the *Billings Gazette* several years later. The newspaper added that soon the hopelessness was apparent even to five of those seven men in the room—all but Siegfriedt and O.H.P. Shelley.

Shelley, a newcomer to town, was like many publishers a political junkie. He'd moved to Red Lodge from Helena, where he'd been accused of rigging the Republican presidential primary election of 1920. Now Shelley could use his political passions on behalf of his town and newspaper. Over the next seven years, he journeyed repeatedly to Washington, D.C., to lobby for the road. He quickly lined up Representative Scott Leavitt, a former Forest Service ranger, as well as Montana senators Thomas Walsh and Burton K. Wheeler. (Some of Siegfriedt's relatives later claimed that although news coverage paints Shelley the lobbyist as the key player, it was Shelley the publisher who wrote that coverage, and it was Siegfriedt's enthusiasm and vitality that held more sway with the powers in Washington.)

Siegfriedt and Shelley did not originally propose the tourist-oriented road we know today. They wanted a small maintenance road. They dreamed of trucks hauling ore from the Cooke City mining districts to a smelter that would be built in Red Lodge. They figured a road for those trucks would cost about $50,000.

However, estimates showed that the road would instead cost $1.14 million (about $15 million in 2012 dollars). If the goal was to build a road from Cooke City to somewhere downhill and closer to civilization, cheaper routes would head down the Stillwater Valley to Columbus ($985,000) or down the

ECONOMIES

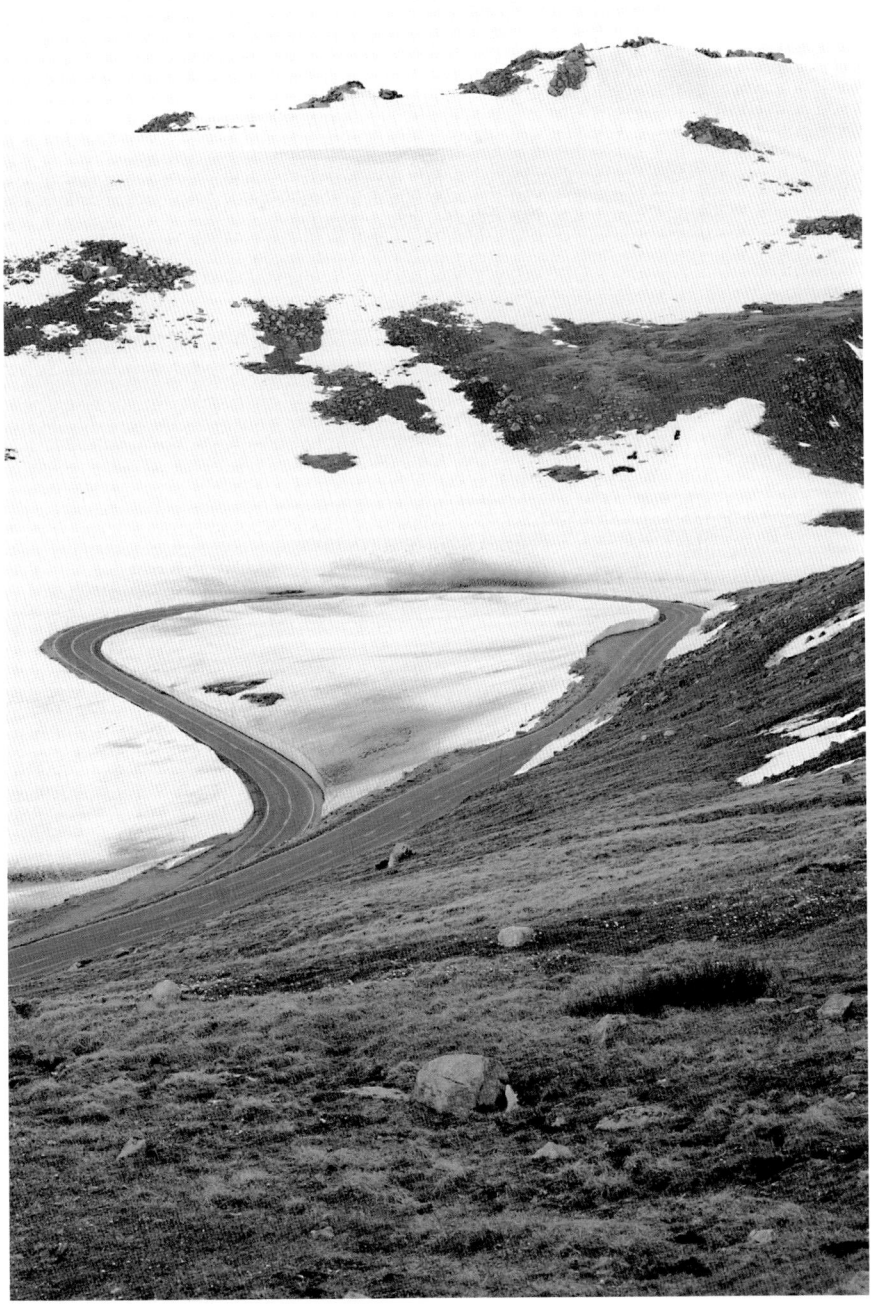

The Beartooth Highway, shown here amid snowdrifts after its late-May opening, was the crazy dream of a group of Red Lodge residents grasping for economic straws after the closing of the coal mines. *Talbot Hauffe/Wyoming Department of Transportation.*

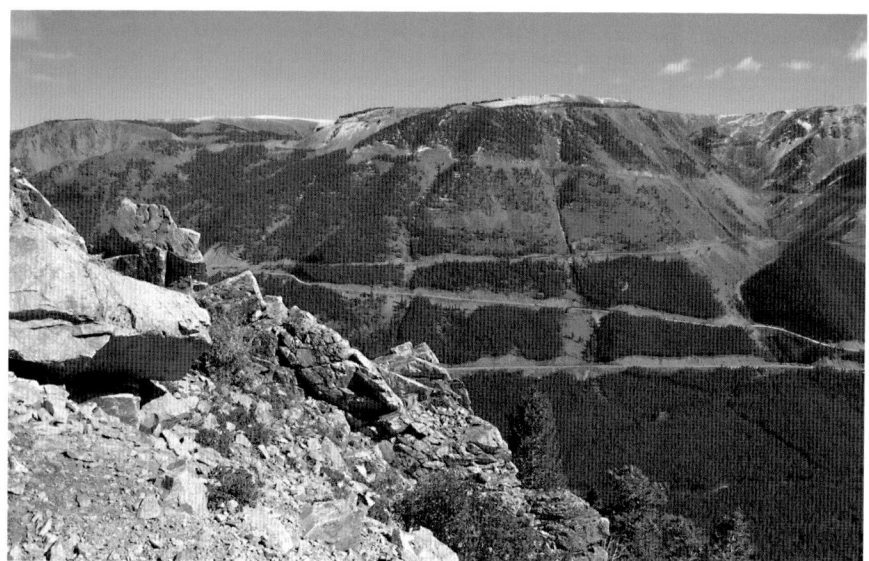

The Beartooth Highway switchbacks south of Red Lodge, shown here from the Hellroaring Road across the valley. This photo was taken in 2005, when the road was closed for reconstruction after mudslides. Groups of construction vehicles are gathered at a couple of points on the right side of the picture. *Courtesy David Kallenbach.*

Clarks Fork valley to Cody, Wyoming ($915,000). A road to Tower Falls in Yellowstone National Park would be cheapest of all at $248,000.

Luckily for Red Lodge, those other communities weren't as active, creative, or effective in lobbying. Shelley, Leavitt, and friends soon realized that the Forest Service would never build such a mining access road, especially at such high cost. So they set their sights instead on the National Park Service.

Cooke City was, of course, situated at the northeast boundary of Yellowstone—a location that wasn't as meaningful back when there were no roads in or out of town. But the Park Service soon started appropriating money to build the road from Cooke to Tower, where it would link with the park loop road. This project meant that the Red Lodge–Cooke City road could serve as an entrance to Yellowstone. Red Lodge boosters regrouped, put their smelter plans on a back burner, and announced that their road's primary value would be to carry tourists to Yellowstone.

Its undeveloped nature thus became a design feature. Planners announced their intention to curtail gas stations, "hot dog stands," summer homes, and hotels. Additionally, no side roads were planned, so that the country could retain its "primitive character." (The word "primitive" was then used to describe qualities today known as "wilderness.")

The project's new goals were aided by engineer Harry Mitchell's 1927 road survey, which chose the route location to maximize scenic panoramas and variety, rather than minimizing altitude or cost. Again, it was a remarkable innovation for the time. Previewing the road just before it opened, the *Gazette* wrote, "Folks who are unused to mountain driving get that hair-raising feeling along the spine when they start up or down the Rock Creek switchbacks. But after the first few turns and a switchback or two they forget their fears and give themselves up to the scenic delights unfolded at every turn."

Leavitt's bill then tied the Beartooth project to funding for other approach roads to national parks around the country. Eligible projects had to be less than sixty miles in length, through territory 90 percent owned by the federal government, and with a primary value of carrying national park travel. By spreading the pork to the home districts of key colleagues, Leavitt and Walsh pushed the bill through the House and Senate in January 1931. President Herbert Hoover signed it into law on January 31, a Saturday night.

From Washington, Shelley wired the news back to his hometown. As the *Red Lodge Picket-Journal* wrote, "Receipt of word that the Presidential signature had been affixed was the signal for an unrestrained celebration centering on Broadway and permeating to every home in the city and community. Telegrams of congratulation and appreciation overflowed the incoming and outgoing wires, a half-dozen impromptu bands were organized, and every noisemaking contrivance in the community was pressed into service." A new era had begun.

Montana Magazine, 2008
Magic City, 2012

Hope and Bacon

In mid-September 1901, a snowstorm blasted the mining camp of Swift Current, located not far from what is now Many Glacier Hotel in Glacier National Park. Fifteen inches of white covered the shacks and tents of town as well as the flecks of gold and copper in the surrounding rock.

Those flecks had drawn miners from places like Butte, where the prospecting days were long passed, and from closer towns—Dupuyer, Choteau, and Great Falls—where settlers still dreamed of riches through a quick strike.

At the turn of the century, Swift Current (also known as Altyn) was one of the last gasps of old-fashioned prospecting fever in Montana—actually, in most of the continental United States. Part of the "ceded strip," it was Blackfeet land that had been recently ceded to mining interests, although conservationists such as George Bird Grinnell would eventually win control of it as part of the park.

And yet what holds fascination for us today is not so much the politics as day-to-day life in the mining camp. To that end, historians have located and reprinted the sole edition of the *Swiftcurrent Courier* newspaper, with its boast that the town would "soon be one of two things, *viz*.: the richest and biggest camp on earth or nothing."

But on this particular snowed-in September morning, as miners settled into a routine that would keep them through the next nine months of winter, another observer was capturing their lives. Philadelphia's female celebrity journalist, pen-named "Suzette," had come to chronicle the frontier. She'd already visited a Blackfeet Indian camp and convinced a guide to take her over Swiftcurrent Pass (perhaps the first woman to make that trek).

Over the next twenty years, Suzette would achieve considerable literary renown under her real name, Caroline Lockhart. Later, however, her star would dim, so few people today are familiar with her portrayals of Swift Current and the other turn-of-the-century Western locales she toured and loved.

Suzette delights in the earthy character of these men she calls *sourdoughs* and in the hardships they endure. About their diet during the blizzard in such terribly remote country, she writes, "I never want to see a piece of bacon again so long as I live."

The camp's food consists primarily of "swine bosom" (her nickname points at how the side pork of that era may not have tasted as divine as today's "bacon") and canned salmon, although Suzette approves of the expectation that "French Pete" might soon steal a beef for the butcher shop. How does she know about this allegedly impending illegal activity? Even a visitor in town knows *everything*. She writes, "There is nothing in the camp to read; no one sews for there is nothing to sew…There is nothing to talk about except that which pertains to mines" and the gossip that covers not only others' activities but even their idle wishes.

Today, in describing such a remote spot as "isolated," we might describe how far you have to drive before you can get cell service or a decent cappuccino. In the Swift Current of 1901, it was two days' ride to the nearest railroad stop, so isolation was woven deep into the community's social fabric. "We live in an ant hill, and the world outside is very big and very far away," Suzette writes. And because it is far away, it is irrelevant. "The Boers might invade England and the news would not awaken a hundredth part of the interest that would the story that Old Man Harris has jumped French Pete's claim."

French Pete has that name to distinguish him from "Swede Pete," who owns a terrier and is one of the later arrivals at the back door of Adlam's saloon for "first drink time." Adlam's is a shack that functions as the community's tavern; it's located almost adjacent to a shack where Suzette is staying, which allows her landlady to provide running commentary on the happy-hour comings and goings. She notes that Old Man Faulkner must be sick again or else he would have been first in line, then "there comes Harris and Bacon Rind Dick. Over there is the judge tearing up the snow like a snowplow…Hofus is late and so is Old Man Boucher. Dear me, my potatoes have burned."

Suzette decides, "As all roads lead to Rome so all trails lead to Adlam's back door. It is a hub from which the paths in the snow run out like the

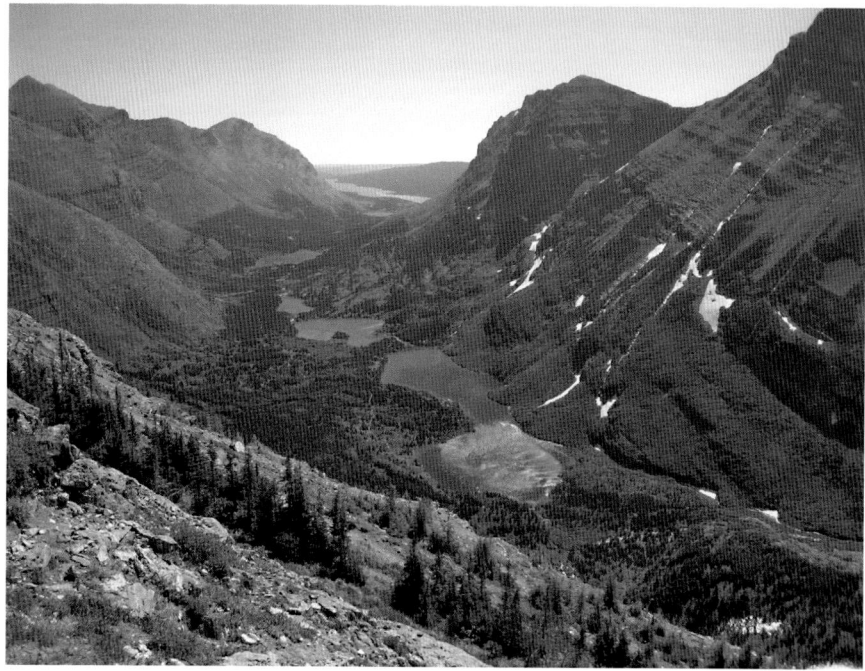

Looking eastward from the top of Swiftcurrent Pass in what is now Glacier National Park, the former mining camp of Swift Current (Altyn) would be in the upper central portion of the photo, under the head of distant Lake Sherburne, hidden by the shoulder of the second mountain from the right. *Courtesy Kari Clayton.*

spokes of a wheel." Then she returns to her breakfast, since it is barely after 7:00 a.m. Adlam's "first drink time," during which the drinks are free, runs from 7:00 to 8:30 a.m.

The men may be there for warmth as much as alcohol. For Suzette, the first action of the morning is "to find a part of the room in which the breezes do not whistle through the cracks where the moss and mud have fallen out." Later, she describes a visit from Old Man Douglas, who "opens the stove door and puts his feet in to bake."

If you're counting, that's four characters so far with the first name "Old Man"—and we haven't even met "Dad" Walker. He's stranded atop the pass without food in the blizzard, and by the time he gets down, five days hence, Suzette will have moved on.

She does get to experience the arrival of two other men who'd been caught without food in the storm, struggling through drifts and blinding snow. As they enter the makeshift inn, they seem at first bewildered. "They have lived alone in the mountains so much that they are shy as the squirrels that peer at one from the pines," she writes. Eventually, "they seem so glad to be warm again…and soon we gather around the table for the noonday meal, with our old friend bacon in the centre."

When Suzette writes that "the isolation and monotony are enough to drive a restless person mad," you get the sense that she is such a restless person—and that most of us today would be as well. But she harbors a tinge of regret for that restlessness and admires the camp residents for the way that "insignificant happenings seem to occupy their minds sufficiently to keep them content."

Then she describes how, after a bacon-heavy dinner, Old Man Douglas walks "through the swirling snow [and] flounders in the drifts across the rickety bridge to his lonely cabin, which is dirty, desolate, and cold. A dreary life for an old man, but he endures it all without complaint for the sake of the 'big stake' he never ceases to believe he is going to make." And you get to wondering what dreariness we today would endure, which dreams would melt our restlessness, and whether we'd have the strength or bullheaded passion to never cease believing in them.

Suzette doesn't venture out to visit anyone's diggings; it is the community, more than its economy, that she grasps as uniquely worth attention. Of course, the mining economy has shaped Montana history in many ways: as a lure to immigrants, a wellspring for innovation, a source of environmental degradation, and a powerful engine of profit. But perhaps none is more significant than the collective attitudes that pervaded the places where these prospectors gathered.

"Hope and bacon keep the camp alive till the Chinook winds blow in the spring and the snow goes out," Suzette writes. "More of them subsist on hope than bacon." Amid the spirit of the mining camp, hope and bacon are such powerful fuels that they speak across the ages, to all of us, a century later, who love the Montana communities that help us balance our restlessness and dreams sufficiently to keep us content.

Montana Quarterly, 2013

Part IV
COMMUNITIES

Mossmain: Montana's Near-Metropolis on the Plains

The story of the '20s, Montana's disastrous decade," wrote beloved historian Joseph Kinsey Howard, was told by "the derelict privy, the boarded-up schoolhouse, the dust-drifted, weed-grown road, and the rotting, rusted fence." This was how the homestead boom of 1900–1917 crashed: year-to-year grain yields could drop by a factor of ten, the average value per acre of farmland fell by 50 percent, and eleven thousand farms (one-fifth of the state total) disappeared entirely.

The tale of the forlorn homesteaders, betrayed by rain that failed to follow the plow, has been often and well told. The realization that Montana's spectacular landscapes could not also become a small farmer's paradise has been seen as a turning point, or even an end point, in the state's history.

But when history focuses solely on the homesteader, we miss the scale of the devastation to the state's image of itself. One way to reveal that scale is to visit the metropolis of Mossmain. Shall we start downtown? Maybe at the Municipal (farmers') Market, next to the Civic Center and City Hall, at one end of the grassy promenade that leads down past the Publishing House to the railroad tracks. From downtown, streets diverge in a fan pattern, and we can stroll down Gardenvale, past schools and play fields toward the tree-lined Institution.

Of course, our stroll must be theoretical, because Mossmain exists only on plans. Nevertheless, its plans—expertly drawn, fully articulated—can tell us a great deal about what leading Montanans of the past expected of their future.

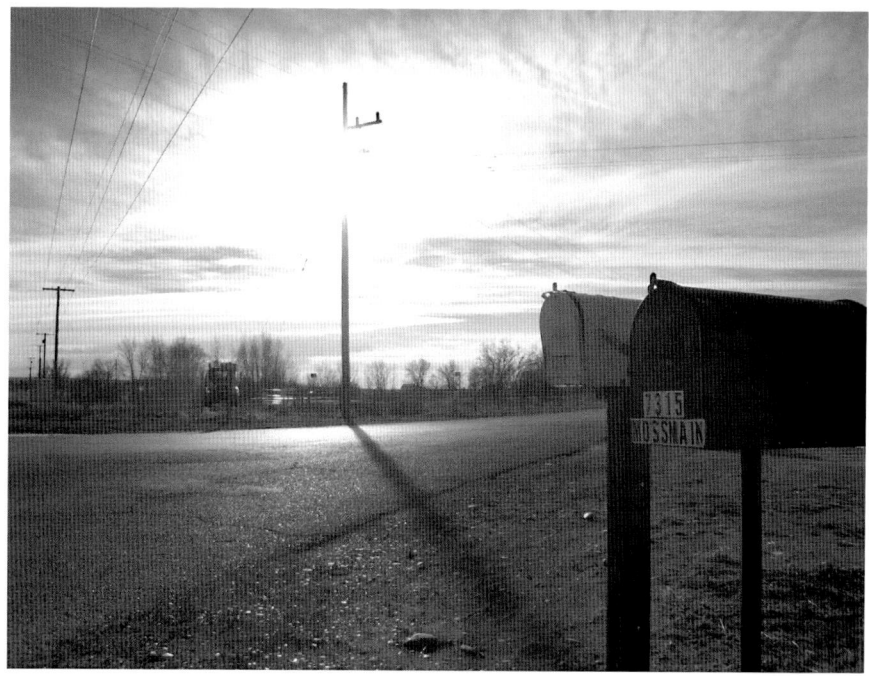

Mossmain once had a post office and metropolis-sized plans. Today, a couple of postal boxes on "Mossmain Lane" in East Laurel are among the few remains of P.B. Moss's dream. *Courtesy Kari Clayton.*

MOSSMAIN WAS THE dream of Preston B. Moss (1863–1947), a Missouri-born financier. Arriving in Billings in 1892, he promptly made $400,000 in the sheep business, emerging from the Panic of 1893 as a major investment force in the state. A prominent banker, he also founded a newspaper, a toothpaste factory, and a meatpacking plant. He helped develop companies that distributed irrigation water, electricity, heat, and telephone service. He co-founded the Northern Hotel and Great Western Sugar Company, and built a 1903 mansion that architectural historian Chere Jiusto has called "one of the finest residences ever built in the state of Montana."

In short, Moss thought big. He was a smart, powerful man who had already helped determine the state's path. He was a "progressive" in a time when progressives were advocating the construction of much of the infrastructure we take for granted today: roads, financial systems, utilities, and eventually airports. He was not always successful: his bank went into receivership in 1910, an action he fought with phrases like "cooked-up deal," implying that regulators had been overly influenced by his competitors. But failure didn't seem to slow him down. His big plans—many called him a "dreamer"—meant that he spent almost his entire life in debt.

After nearly two decades in Billings, Moss apparently decided he could do better. Sure, Billings was on the railroad, but fourteen miles west of Billings was the intersection of *three* railroads: the Northern Pacific going east–west along the Yellowstone River, plus the Great Northern hooking into northern networks via Judith Gap and Great Falls and the Burlington hooking into southern networks via Worland and Casper. At this spot, near the hamlet of Laurel, the Northern Pacific had just established the largest terminal yards between Minneapolis and Seattle. Moss knew that being located at such a rail junction meant cheap rates and fast service. He also foresaw the Panama Canal creating demand for a new rail corridor from Galveston through Denver and Mossmain to Seattle. Such forces, he likely knew, had driven the explosive growth of nineteenth-century cities such as Chicago. So as receivership forced him to step down from the bank in 1910, he decided to create a new such metropolis.

Moss took his new city very seriously. He traveled to Europe for research, and developed a philosophy that would guide development. Mossmain would be "the first garden city in America," he declared. The Garden City movement, which had originated in Letchworth, England, in 1903, was designed to put "every home in a garden setting, not a vegetable garden alone, but ample gardens adorned with flowers, shrubbery, and shade trees."

The Industrial Revolution had created an ugly dichotomy. Cities brimmed with tenements so grim and dismal that many residents were drawn to communism as a desirable alternative. Meanwhile, small farms such as those in eastern Montana lacked most emerging technologies (plumbing, electricity, telephones) but suffered even more from isolation, with each farm being located far from neighbors and communities.

Moss's utopian plan, then, was to integrate agriculture and urban life, not only through gardens "to relieve the nerve tension of city life" but also by creating a city that would make intensive farming in the wider area more profitable, desirable, and social. A "farmer's wife and children should not be deprived of the conveniences of Modern Home Life," he wrote.

The city would also improve farm economics. With a "value-added" philosophy, Moss believed that Montana should develop industry to turn its agricultural products into finished goods. For example, he believed the Mossmain area would be particularly good for apple orchards (and indeed, to this day you find remnants of orchards up the Clarks Fork of the Yellowstone)—but he also believed that Mossmain should have a facility to turn those apples into applesauce. Mossmain would thus gain advantage from the surrounding farms, just as the farms would from the nearby metropolis.

Pursuing the Garden City concept required an aggressive effort at urban planning and community management. Moss said these actions were justified because "we of America have not made a great success of our city building," with too much financial speculation and not enough attention to citizens' social lives and leisure. For example, with a Montana commitment to classlessness, Moss proposed "Club Houses for men and women without regard to previous social condition"; during the run-up to Prohibition, it was seen as an additional mark of healthy progressivism that these clubhouses would replace saloons.

To express his philosophy on the ground, Moss turned to Chicago architect Walter Burley Griffin. An associate of Frank Lloyd Wright, Griffin had designed several well-received buildings of the Midwestern Prairie School style. But now he was increasingly turning to landscapes—and was suddenly famous for them. In 1912, he won a contest to design the brand-new Australian capital city of Canberra, a contest that

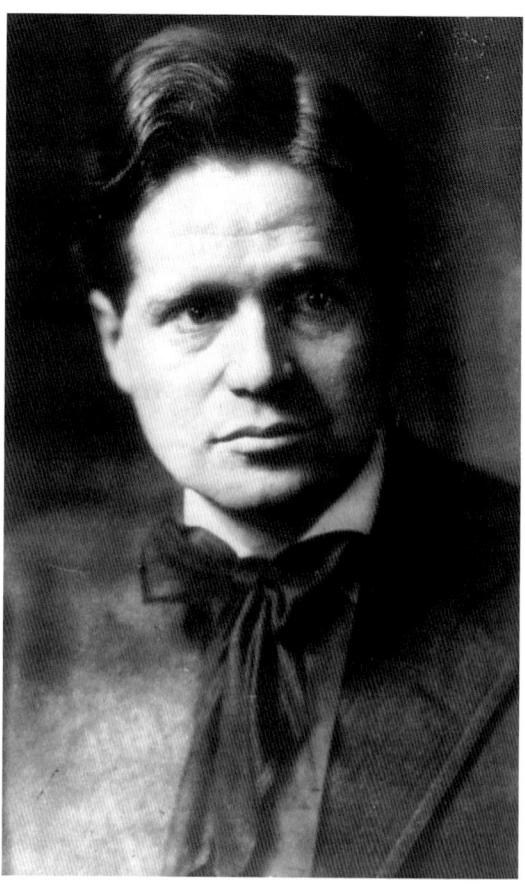

Walter Burley Griffin, a Chicago-based associate of Frank Lloyd Wright, won a prestigious international contest to design the new capital of Australia—and then planned a similar metropolis, Mossmain, for Montana. *Library of Congress LC-USZ62-59749.*

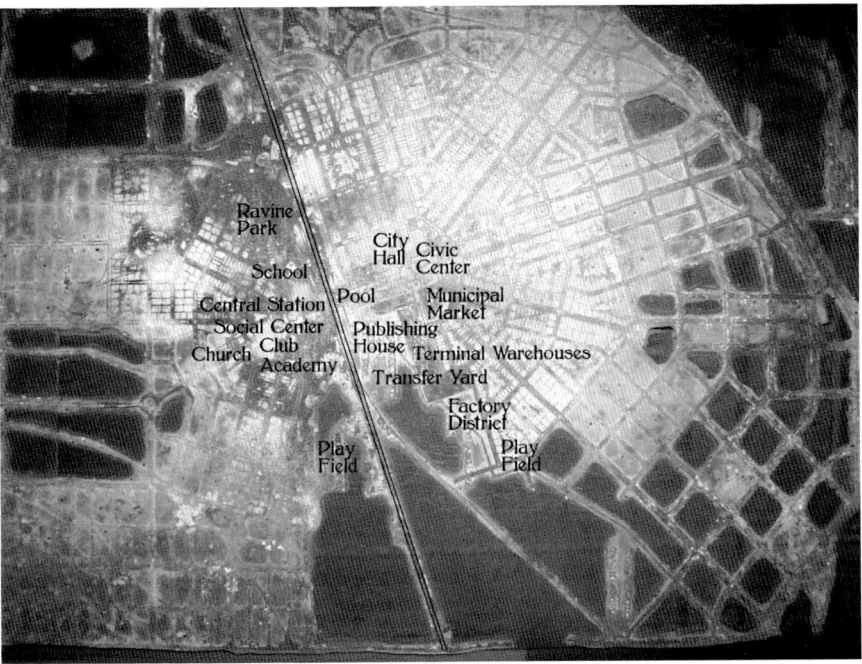

The plan of Mossmain, Montana, as drawn by Walter Burley Griffin. The city is bisected by the Northern Pacific railroad tracks, which run roughly parallel to today's I-90. *Taken from a metal printing plate courtesy of the Moss Mansion, with annotations by Kari Clayton.*

Griffin's biographers, Mati Maldre and Paul Kruty, quote one of his clients as calling "perhaps the greatest international competition in the history of the world for city planning and architecture." In 1913, Griffin visited Australia, and on his way home he met P.B. Moss at Mossmain.

In a later lecture, Griffin gave equal time to his plans for the Australian capital and the "railroad center of an orchard region" in Montana. Both were complete civic units that considered climate (sunlight, winds, water supply, beauty) and community in balance. His Mossmain plans provided for terminal warehouse facilities, stockyards, a packinghouse, and a cold storage and creamery plant, but they also included a radial street system with plenty of parks, playgrounds, and open spaces. It was an ideal Midwestern Garden City, a chance to build a new, better Chicago on a new frontier.

Moss, armed with the plans though not yet an official plat, set out to raise money. His idealism may have hampered his results with investors: he bragged that Mossmain would "reverse the usual city building methods which have to do with town lot speculation schemes." There would be little buying and selling of land; instead, Mossmain farms and businesses would hold long-term leases on their land, which would remain in the ownership of a vague collective. (In the 1910s, socialist ideals were not yet fully discredited in this country—but potential investors probably frowned.)

Moss did successfully lure a magazine publisher to relocate from Lincoln, Nebraska, to his planned publishing house. Until it could be built, Richard Haste published the *Scientific Farmer* from offices in Billings, assisted by his twenty-five-year-old daughter, Gwendolen, and a secretary, Cora Fleming.

And then—nothing happened. Nobody invested. Moss built a small house in Mossmain and finagled a post office for the community in 1917. (Fleming served as postmistress, although she resented having to live out in the middle of nowhere.) But Moss's grand plans withered. The commonly accepted story blames the advent of World War I.

YET SOMETHING ELSE happened in 1917 that was likely a far more significant obstacle to Mossmain. That year was the beginning of Montana's devastating drought. And the drought, with the accompanying realization that the previous fifteen years had been abnormally wet, sparked the homesteaders' exodus. It marked the slow, sad, culture-wide realization that Montana was not the Midwest, would not fill up with small farms, and would not follow the path from empty frontier to intensively cultivated civilization that had marked the history of everywhere east of the 100th meridian.

And yet if Montana couldn't become a Midwestern farming paradise, neither could it develop Midwestern-style cities. The Mossmain prospectus had bragged, "When this territory shall have been developed in the same per capita ratio per square mile as in Ohio or Indiana, it will have a total population of 1,600,000." Within a radius of a hundred miles, Moss expected, the rural population alone would top 500,000, with several large cities accounting for the rest.

Those cities, Moss expected, would be powered by outfits like *The Scientific Farmer*, which promoted the Campbell system of dry farming—the very system many homesteaders blamed for exacerbating the drought. In addition to applesauce factories, Moss envisioned an agricultural school "similar to those operating in Belgium, Holland, and Denmark [aimed at] making the small truck farm profitable." In other words, the rural boom would fuel an urban boom, and eventually southern Montana would look just like Greater Chicago.

But if the rural boom was predicated on faulty assumptions—that dry farming could support hundreds of thousands of homesteaders—then so was the equally longed-for urban boom. Thus, as the homesteaders' dream was smashed, so too was the dream of urban Montana's future.

Today, Montana is rightly proud of its ghost towns, which are usually a set of abandoned structures in the middle of nowhere. Mossmain is different in two ways: first, it was never built. Second, as Billings and Laurel creep closer to each other, it's in the middle of somewhere. What would have been Mossmain is now the Interstate 90 East Laurel exit, a drive-in movie theater, a chemical distributor, and a horse arena.

The people involved in the story likewise moved on to other functions. P.B. Moss ran for Congress in 1922 on an agricultural platform, losing to an opponent backed by the Anaconda company (and thus all of the state's newspapers). He also lost his Billings mansion to foreclosure, though its subsequent restoration has since burnished his reputation. Walter Burley Griffin moved permanently to Australia, where he is now considered one of the leading architect-planners in that country's history. Gwendolen Haste, daughter of the magazine publisher, became a noted New York City poet who often wrote about the Montana homesteaders she had met.

In retrospect, perhaps the failure of Mossmain was good news. It might have been a terrible modern city: planned without anticipation of advances in railroads, refrigeration, and automobile traffic. Meanwhile, the thwarted dreams of the 1920s helped shape the resilient character of all who lived through those difficult days. Montanans of the 1920s and '30s, unable to simply replicate the Midwest, struggled to build an economy and culture unique to the state. Their successes and failures create a heritage that benefits everyone who lives here today, more so than any city might have, no matter how beautifully planned.

Montana Magazine, 2013

Community, Enriched by Formula

In 1997, we marked the fiftieth anniversary of the official death of a dusty pocket of Western history known by the bland and oddly capitalized name of "The Montana Study." Most people—even most Montanans—have never heard of it.

Many of those who *have* heard of The Montana Study—devotees of rural sociology, community organizers with an academic background, or the sorts of intellectuals who love to talk about small towns but would never dream of living in one—revere it. Some even cite it as a vital precursor to the civil rights movement. Others make a stronger case that today's "community movement" has important roots in The Montana Study.

The Montana Study is heralded as the nation's first conscious attempt to improve the quality of rural life by strengthening a sense of community. It upheld the values of neighborliness, belonging, and face-to-face democracy. It was an effort to conquer the frontier—especially the social and cultural frontier—with town meetings.

It spawned numerous philosophies, ideas, and techniques still in use by community advocates. Its organizers insisted on frank but friendly discussion, cooperative research, and constructive problem-solving. They emphasized participation by a wide variety of townspeople, with large committee meetings supplemented by specialized task forces. They encouraged local residents to envision the future, set goals, and believe in the power of local people to achieve those goals.

The nuts and bolts of its "Ten-week Study Guide" could still work today: Why do I live in this community? Who are the people and institutions that make up this community? What is our economic base? How does our town relate to the state and the nation? What do we see for the future and how do we get there? And finally, what have we accomplished and where do we go next?

In 1943, University of Montana chancellor Ernest Melby and David Stevens of the Rockefeller Foundation began a community development service—though perhaps in deference to Melby's academic position, or because the concept was still so new, they called it a "study." Melby recruited Northwestern University philosophy professor Baker Brownell as director, with two half-time staff people, sociologist Paul Meadows and Great Falls writer Joseph Kinsey Howard.

The service's first project came in Lonepine, a spot near Hot Springs, west of Flathead Lake, then consisting of a general store, a dirt road, and a few residences. Because Lonepine had not been settled until 1910, many of the original settlers were still there, growing old, watching young people move away, watching themselves be left behind by progress. They responded to Brownell's rhetoric that rural communities provided "the best conditions for wholesome living…the only atmosphere in which democracy can thrive and remain a powerful force in our country."

To the surprise of many, the town's initial fervor endured: residents enlisted discussion leaders and research committees; they generated historical documents and economic development reports; they put on celebratory banquets and even a historical pageant directed by a professor from the state college in Bozeman, who had been brought on as another Montana Study staffer.

Other communities signed on as well: working through the study guide, holding discussions, putting on pageants, and forming action teams on localized issues. Over the next four years, the study initiated half a dozen programs in the western and central portions of the state. The staff's lectures, articles, and books were fairly well received in national academic circles. But the study also developed huge internal problems.

Melby moved on to New York University. Brownell completed his term and returned to Northwestern. Meadows switched over to teaching full time. Howard, citing the demands of his writing career, also left. By 1947, the study was in the hands of Bert Hansen, the drama professor; Ruth Robinson, who had been an ardent volunteer in the study group in Conrad; and Frank Smith, newly hired from Kentucky as an expert in community recreation and country dance.

Furthermore, the Rockefeller grant ran out; the 1947 plan was for the state university system to appropriate another $50,000 for two more years of the study. But enacting such a plan was an utterly political task, and the study had no political capital. Its leaders alienated the other university campuses by running everything out of Missoula. Melby attempted widespread reform of the university system, and his departure was prompted by losing that battle with the state legislature. Howard, the outspoken author of *High, Wide, and Handsome*, continued to publish magazine articles critical of "the Company"—the Anaconda Copper Mining Company, which thoroughly controlled the state's politics. And the entire staff was constantly battling charges that the study must be some form of communism.

In a feat of backroom politics that leaves unclear who precisely was responsible, the 1947 legislature emerged with a university appropriation that did not include The Montana Study. In July of that year its offices shut down.

WHEN HE ASKED me to write this article, *Chronicle of Community* editor Don Snow cited the "first-ness" of The Montana Study. "What intrigues me is the impulse to do it at all," Don said. "These were people who realized the implications of de-occupying the countryside, not only in terms of wrecked communities, but our national identity, which is wrapped in a sentimental view of rural and agrarian life. And they thought about heading it off, or at least addressing its implications. They were the first to try to puzzle together this notion of rural vitality, a notion that over these fifty years has grown to a sizable industry."

On the other hand, Luther Propst of the Sonoran Institute, who seeks to empower small, scenic communities throughout the Rocky Mountain West, is skeptical about first-ness. "Many Southern states (and probably elsewhere, but I saw this growing up in the South) carried out similar efforts to promote schools, public facilities, and infrastructure in the postwar environment," he told me. "It was part of the optimism of the day and a desire to create jobs for war heroes. In those days, there was probably more of a sense of community and shared future for white middle-class veterans with aspirations for raising a family."

Advocates of The Montana Study might counter that it started before the end of the war, and that even if you want to view it as part of a nationwide movement, it's still a remarkably admirable impulse. The people in Lonepine and other isolated Montana towns: they thought they could improve their lives. They thought this despite remoteness in an increasingly cosmopolitan world, despite the Company, despite backward facilities and limping economies and dwindling population—despite, in other words, whatever hardships the world would throw at them. And diving into the work, the study, they—at least some of them—enjoyed it. *They enjoyed it.* They allowed this vague notion of community improvement to shape their hobbies, careers, dreams, ideals, philosophies. And they felt fulfilled by that.

Propst can skewer that romanticism as well. "Let's not let our desire to write a nostalgic, community-based history for Montana gloss over the role of Anaconda and other forces of colonialism," he said. On the other hand, Propst today shares these tools and philosophies with communities around the West; despite his skepticism about the significance of the impulse, he's living proof of the endurance of those themes.

WHAT DID THE study accomplish? In Lonepine, residents spoke of an increased sense of history, an ability to think objectively, and an appreciation of their community. Nothing you can exactly show to a state legislator, like you might a dam or a highway or some other piece of concrete, and say, "That's why I want $50,000." In other communities, the record was mixed: Darby focused attention on a new lumber mill, Stevensville started an adult education program, Conrad passed a bond issue to expand the high school, and Lewistown initiated a series of folk-dancing programs.

The historical record is thoroughly confused because the study's chief legacy—its edifice that may well last as long as any concrete—is a book that trumpets its results. Richard Poston, who'd been a sort of study groupie, published *Small Town Renaissance* in 1950. It is a magnificently odd book, powerful and sublime and underwhelming and dull all at the same time. In his opening paragraph, Poston sets both his ambition and his insistent capitalization scheme: "I am convinced that in this experiment, known as The Montana Study, there is to be found a secret by which people throughout all America, rich or poor, educated or uneducated, can make their lives richer, more enjoyable, and more worth while." He interviews people in all the participating communities, and they issue glowing reports. But his writing style, reminiscent of a '30s newsreel narration, loans a flourish to notions that might otherwise seem self-evident, even commonplace. And he is so obviously partisan that you can't help wondering where his enthusiasm might have trumped the reasoned analysis so valued by his subject.

Poston and his book—more than Melby, Brownell, or any individual in any of the communities that did the actual work—created the underground cult of The Montana Study. Worn copies of *Small Town Renaissance* got handed around at conferences, taught at obscure colleges in the Midwest, and pored over as gospel.

Now eighty-two, Richard Poston lives in Houston, where "I have now retired for the fourth time, and am writing my seventh book," he told me in a crisply typed three-page letter. "The Montana Study led to the creation of my career which as indicated below, has influenced thousands of people in various communities in the United States and other countries." In his career, Poston created community development field services at the University of Washington and Southern Illinois University; he wrote, lectured, and consulted internationally.

But—much to my surprise, given his reputation for dogged optimism—he is less enthusiastic about the legacy of the study itself. Indeed, when I pressed him on that subject, he wrote back, "Although I hate to say it, you might as well face up to the fact that the 'tools' of The Montana Study as you put it, are not being applied nationwide. The reasons why are too numerous to get into."

ONE PERSON WHO disagrees about that legacy grew up playing basketball in a gym in Libby, Montana. The gym had been built largely through the efforts of the Greater Libby Association, an outgrowth of the study. The young basketball player carried his debt of gratitude into middle age and into his job as governor. In fact, Marc Racicot told me in a telephone interview, "I'm not sure that any reflection of history has had more impact on me, in terms of both historical lessons and inspiration." It was so important to him that he urged all members of his top management team to read *Small Town Renaissance*. "While we manage the state's daily affairs, which is no small task," he said, "we also need to look beyond tomorrow. The lessons of The Montana Study are that we must be willing to take those risks and must have faith that people are innately good and will act for the benefit of the community."

Libby is an interesting case study—and not only because of who grew up there. The Greater Libby Association attempted one of the study's most ambitious goals. In addition to institutional buildings, its focus became a sixty-year sustained-yield agreement under which the local mill would turn over management of its timber lands to the government in exchange for a guaranteed yearly cut. "It represented remarkable potential trust among these entities: private business, labor, local, state, and federal governments," Racicot said. "We might today think their numbers were slightly off, but it was a far-reaching, insightful analysis. Today, you couldn't try something like that, with the various political pressures. But Libby might have been better off, both economically and environmentally, if that sustained-yield agreement had come together."

It did not come together, Racicot believes, because there was no urgency. The future was too far away. This is a theme that he and many other of the study's supporters continually return to: planning for the future. Amid the turmoil of your everyday life, to envision your community twenty years from now requires great courage; to act on that vision requires great wisdom; to complete those actions...well, it's hardly ever done. But the legacy of The Montana Study, supporters suggest, is an example of coming damn close.

Chronicle of Community, 1997

IN THE GARDEN OF EDEN

Today, Bearcreek is known mostly as the site of a 1943 coal-mining disaster or as a place where you can bet on pig races. When you ask almost anyone in Bearcreek about why they live there, they'll cite the peace and quiet. But in 1926, the windswept, sage-covered spot on the eastern slopes of the Beartooth Mountains was alleged to have been—quite literally—the Garden of Eden.

The peace and quiet shouldn't be surprising, given that Bearcreek had just thirty-seven residents in the 1990 census, making it the smallest city in the state. (Ismay, with twenty-one residents, is organized as a town rather than a city.) But in the early part of the twentieth century, with five coal mines regularly filling railroad cars, the Bearcreek area was home to almost three thousand people.

Frank DeVille arrived in Bearcreek at age two and stayed. He worked in agriculture and mining and as a county commissioner. In 1993, at age eighty-one, he talked about the community's out-of-the-way quality, where neighbors aren't too close. Then he described the city as it was when he grew up: "We had a theater, two hotels, hardware stores, clothing stores, a lumberyard, cafés, restaurants, a drugstore with a nickelodeon you could dance to, three hospitals, a bowling alley…and saloons—it seemed every other building was a saloon."

It was a close-knit town, he said. Miners would "have arguments and then be friends the next day. Good friends even after a fight. You had to be good friends working in the mine." They would all get together for

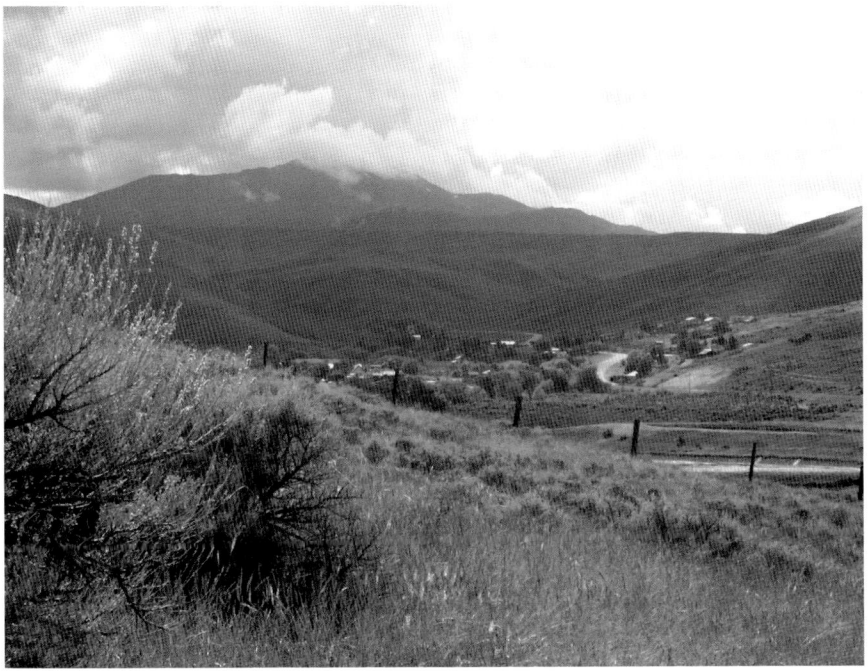

The hamlet of Bearcreek, shown here looking west from the cemetery in June 2009, is quiet today—but was once a thriving coal-mining city. *Courtesy Kari Clayton.*

a baseball tournament on Labor Day and to put on a party for the kids at Christmas.

That lifestyle ended in two ways—gradually and then suddenly, as the old joke goes. The sudden part was the Smith Mine Disaster. At 10:00 a.m. on February 27, 1943, an accumulation of methane gas was ignited by a miner wearing an open light. This set off the coal dust, and the explosion rocked much of the mine's #3 seam. Many miners were killed in the blast, and others were trapped, facing inescapable death from carbon monoxide poisoning. The rescue crew found messages chalked onto pieces of powder boxes: "We tried to do our best but we couldn't get out"; "I'm sorry we had to go this way. God bless you all"; "Wifes and daughters: we died an easy death. Love from us both. Be good."

It was the worst coal-mining accident in the state's history: seventy-four of the seventy-seven men in the crew died, and a rescue worker died three weeks later from the effects of the gas.

The city never recovered. Yet the gradual part, DeVille recalled, was that the economy "had been going downhill for a good many years before the disaster. They were losing contracts for coal as people switched to other fuels." The Washoe, International, and Bearcreek mines had already closed, and now the Smith, with the valley's best coal, would not reopen. The Foster and Brophy mines held on a bit longer, and the Janskovitch brothers, Frank and Polie, ran a two-man operation until 1970, when federal regulations shut them down. But "the disaster" (as residents call it) marked the point at which Bearcreek changed.

"After the disaster, people sold their places for peanuts," DeVille said. Many of the downtown buildings were torn down, and houses were moved to sites up and down the nearby valley of the Clarks Fork of the Yellowstone River.

And so today it is quiet. The two-mile stretch between Bearcreek and the community of Washoe, once covered with houses, is now empty. Remnants of the old mining operations dot the valley: obviously abandoned, they give it a ghostly, forlorn appearance.

The ghostly image fades a bit as you enter Bearcreek proper. Several homes remain, along with the Bear Creek Saloon (site of the pig races) and the post office—open mornings only.

Postmistress Ann Lose said she likes the quiet and the peacefulness. "It's a treat to have your kids roam the hills. And they can still get on a bus to Belfry [for school]. It's a good place to raise kids—we can keep a pretty good eye on them."

"There's a lot of stability here," she continued, "a lot of old-timers. I'm a relative newcomer." She'd been in Bearcreek fifteen years.

These people enjoy their neighbors, but given the scarcity of humans in town, they also appreciate the land. Threse Fuchs said she loves the peaceful, quiet quality of Bearcreek. She also liked the warmth. "The growing season is longer than in Red Lodge," she says. "It's much easier to have a garden."

Bearcreek is set amid rolling terrain under the big sky that has made Montana famous. In some ways it marks a transition between the eastern and western regions of the state: the valley is dry, open rangeland, but it backs up to tall, forested Mount Maurice, the eastern tip of the Beartooth Range.

"It's like living in a dry ocean," Fuchs said. "When you look at the terrain, you can see where the water would have been. It's just beautiful."

For Frank DeVille, the land means good hunting. "We're up in the foothills," he said, "where the hunting is ideal, or used to be. We've had pheasants, sage hens, and grouse. When I was a kid we ate a lot of rabbits. You didn't need a license or anything then—I'd bring along a gun when I went to tend cattle, catch a rabbit or two for dinner."

But more than the land or the people, residents said that it's history that defines Bearcreek. "It has a ghostly vibe with all the history," Fuchs says. "That's where the peacefulness comes from."

On a warm October day, DeVille had been working in his basement. "I'm changing my coal furnace to butane," he said. Fifty years after the disaster, the DeVilles and several other residents still heated their houses with coal. "We have to go [120 miles] to Roundup to get the coal, and we decided, now that we're getting on in years, maybe won't be quite as mobile, it might be nice to have something easier."

He was obviously making the change with some reluctance. Like his hometown, DeVille had been shaped and enriched by the legacy of the coal mines. "I do still like that coal heat," he said.

THE GARDEN OF EDEN notion started, like so much else in Bearcreek, with Dr. J.C.F. Siegfriedt (introduced previously as the Father of the Beartooth Highway). One day in 1926, Siegfriedt examined a piece of carbonaceous shale on the top of a loaded coal car coming out of Bearcreek's Eagle mine. Encrusted in the rock was a mammalian tooth. The miners thought it looked exactly like a recently extracted molar. Siegfriedt agreed.

The enamel had turned to carbon and the lime of the roots to iron, but when Siegfriedt showed it to dentists and fossil enthusiasts in Billings, they too agreed: it was a tooth of a primitive human. Furthermore, it dated back to earlier than either Neanderthal Man or Java Man, which were then the oldest human bones known to paleontology.

They could date the Bearcreek Tooth so precisely because they knew where it had come from: a dark-colored, clay-like layer just above the Eagle Mine's Seam 3. It was fifteen feet above the base of the Fort Union formation, among deposits laid down in the Eocene period, about thirty-five to fifty-five million years ago, during the emergence of the first modern mammals. Already that layer had produced fossils including fish scales, turtle scutes (a turtle's hard exterior plates), and shark teeth.

But a human tooth was something different—especially in the hands of Dr. Siegfriedt. "He was the epitome of the booster," Thomas Lewis recalled in a historical essay. When Siegfriedt served as mayor of Red Lodge in the 1930s, "Many a visitor was stopped on the street or invited out of his car to be welcomed to the town by the mayor himself." Siegfriedt was thus the kind of man who would publicize a paleontological discovery in outlets beyond the scholarly journals. Within days of the discovery, articles on the Bearcreek Tooth

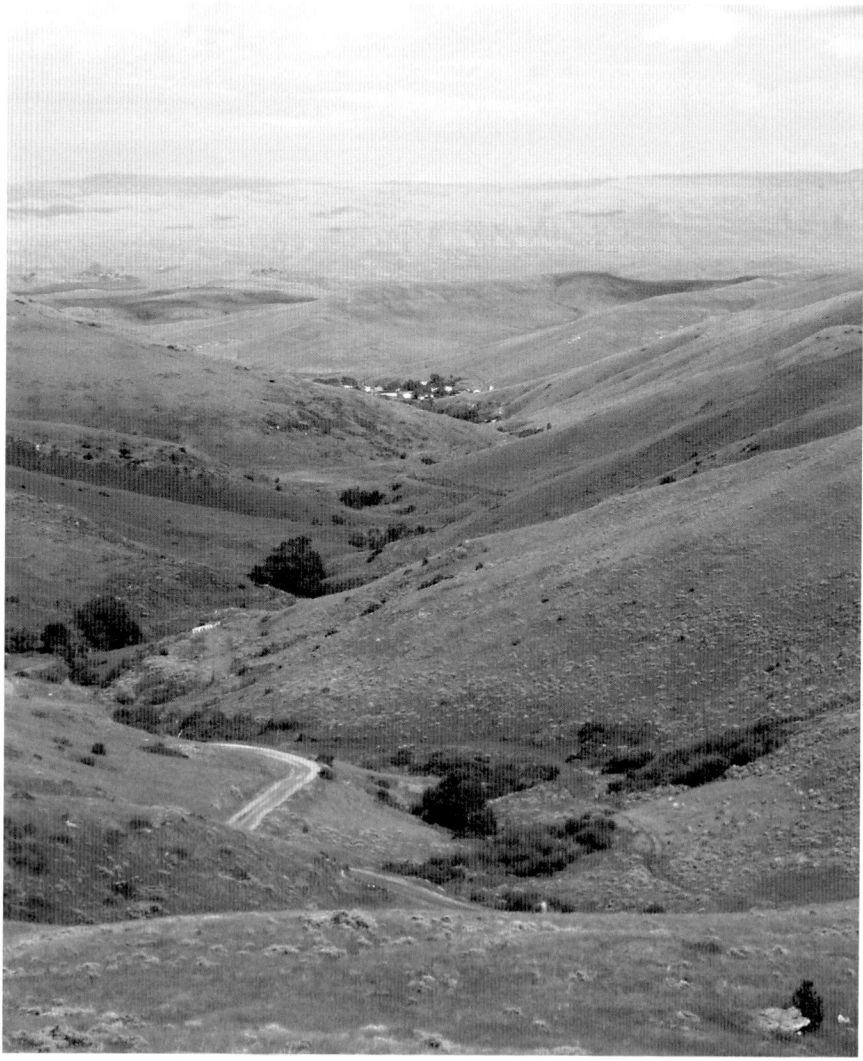

Bearcreek, shown here in the middle distance, can be quite scenic after the spring rains. But could it really have been the Garden of Eden? *Courtesy Kari Clayton.*

appeared in publications as distant as the *New York Times*. Siegfriedt pitched reporters with an interpretive leap that would make any booster proud. He said that if the Bearcreek Tooth was the oldest known human fossil, then Bearcreek had to be the place where human life began: the Garden of Eden.

This line of thinking was of nationwide interest at the time because the discovery came on the heels of the famed Scopes Monkey Trial of 1925.

A Tennessee teacher had been accused of teaching evolution, in violation of state law, and his trial featured two of the era's most famous lawyers, three-time presidential candidate William Jennings Bryan versus prominent trial attorney Clarence Darrow. The trial was something of a publicity stunt: defendant John Scopes had volunteered to be prosecuted so that local businessmen could profit from the descent of more than two hundred journalists to tiny Dayton, Tennessee. But the publicity indeed galvanized forces pro and con; nationwide, in the trial's aftermath, forty-one bills or resolutions were introduced in state legislatures to mimic the Tennessee anti-evolution law.

So the entire country was debating human evolution. Could human teeth be contained in rocks? What did that imply about the biblical version of history? Could Bible and science be merged in a way that would put the Garden of Eden at the site of the oldest known human bone? And—best of all for a booster's purposes—might that spot be in a relatively undeveloped region of Montana?

Unfortunately there was one slight problem, which came to light over the next several months. The tooth wasn't human. It turned out to be from a condylarth, a now-extinct creature that looked a little like a raccoon. Condylarths, as ancestors of hoofed mammals and perhaps the first herbivorous mammals, are of great interest to evolutionary biologists. But to the general public, they're far less glamorous than the prospect of "Bearcreek Man."

A funny thing happened, though, on the way to this disappointment: Siegfriedt fell in love with paleontology. He realized that he loved finding and examining bones in rocks, whether they were potentially human or not. He continued his communications with nationally known scientists, calling himself, with tongue in cheek, a Paleontologist-at-Large and the self-appointed president of the apocryphal Beartooth University.

The Bearcreek area proved to have many interesting fossils, and if the Bearcreek Tooth did not spawn a rush of settlers to spur area growth, it did attract geologists to spur the doctor's intellect. North of Bearcreek in 1930, members of a Princeton University expedition found fragments of a dinosaur egg shell, the first such find in North America. When they showed the fragments to Siegfriedt, "his ecstasy was explosive and uncontrollable," expedition leader Glenn Jepsen later recalled.

Jepsen and other leaders of that expedition soon formalized a more permanent group, the Yellowstone Bighorn Research Association (YBRA). After a few years of working out of buildings Siegfriedt owned south of Red

Lodge, YBRA built its own camp on the slopes of Mount Maurice—where it continues to this day to provide college students with a firsthand view of millions of years of geology. "In a sense," YBRA's website says, "Jepsen's long career in the Fort Union faunas of the Bighorn Basin confirmed [Siegfriedt's] idea of [Bearcreek as] a cradle of evolution."

Today budding scientists come to the YBRA camp to deepen their understanding of the past and the present. It's a far cry from the reasons that drew most people to Montana in the frontier days. Then, mere rumors of a gold strike or productive farmland were enough to draw hordes of eager settlers—so much so that a skilled publicist was any community's most valuable asset. But as the region and society at large matured and fact replaced rumor, regional prosperity has come to increasingly depend on hard-nosed science.

The Bearcreek Tooth may not have been the key to unlocking the Garden of Eden, and it may not have had much effect on the peace and quiet that today's Bearcreekers value. But it did spur much productive paleontology and the founding of a valuable scientific community. In this sense, Siegfriedt's enthusiastic new discoveries constituted a personal evolution—from booster to scientist—that represents an entire state coming out of its frontier phase to find its modern identity.

Montana Magazine, 1993 and 2009

The Teenaged West

In Gardiner, Montana, I asked the teenagers for adjectives to describe their lives.

"Boring," one called out, and I sensed some mythologizing going on. The kid knew that teenagers are supposed to be disaffected, jaded, bored. It was a cloak he could easily don: *sure, I'm just another bored teenager.* By pretending to be bored, he wouldn't have to work very hard—and who knows, then it might turn into a self-fulfilling prophecy.

He may also have been testing me: many grown-ups get infuriated at the notion that teenagers are bored. They say, "How can you be bored when surrounded by beautiful mountains like this?" Then they go away and leave the teenagers alone. I decided to just write "Bored" on the chalkboard and hold the chalk to wait for another adjective.

"Desolate," said somebody else, along the same lines. But then we got down to business.

"Mountains," said somebody; "wildlife," said another; "sagebrush," said a third. These weren't adjectives, but I didn't want to get hung up on grammatical rules. Not when I had a chance to learn about the lives of rural teenagers.

"Driving": the kids drove everywhere. "Basketball": the Gardiner boys' team was currently advancing in the state playoffs. "Skiing," "snowboarding," "hunting," "desert," "drought."

I was there to talk to them about Mildred Walker's novel *Winter Wheat*, in a statewide program sponsored by the Montana Committee for the Humanities. I was afraid they'd find the novel boring. I'd actually found it a little bit boring myself, until about halfway through when its carefully layered construction built up enough momentum to propel me to the end.

At best, I hoped, comparing the novel to their own experiences would make it less boring for them—at least, less boring than my high school English classes had been for me. At worst, I'd learn something about what it was like to grow up in rural Montana in the twenty-first century.

The book is set on a 1940s Montana wheat farm, and I asked them for similar one-word descriptions of the lives of its characters.

"Boring," the same wag said, and we all laughed.

But soon we came up with a list: prairie, quiet, cold, wheat, community, deadly, spare time.

With it going so well, I decided to test out a theory of mine. "How many of you are familiar with cowboy novels?" I asked. "John Wayne movies?"

Enough nodded their heads that I plunged in. "Let's do the same for those."

Our results: outlaws, romantic relationships, action (in the sense of violence), sheriffs, suspense. Mindful of "community" on the previous list, I suggested adding "individualism" to this one; they agreed. It was a bit more vague, since we weren't examining a specific text, but it still looked remarkably different from the other lists.

The lists demonstrated that in the real West—now or sixty years ago—outlaws, sheriffs, and romantic relationships are not terribly significant. The deadliness comes only from weather and driving. But the tie to landscape is deeper and more rewardingly complicated than moviemakers portray.

This difference between movies and real life is not surprising and has often been written about. Of course, no Hollywood genre fits people's actual lives. Your love life is nothing like a romantic comedy, that classroom was nothing like *Dead Poets' Society*, and reality is nothing like reality television.

At the same time, however, everyone in our culture understands the themes of cowboy books and movies. We all know that iconic set of adjectives. We quickly grasp those mythologized images. They're an easy set of stereotypes.

So when we as Westerners interact with "the grown-ups" (governments, corporations, environmental organizations, "Easterners," "Californians," anyone we see as being from that other culture that seeks to control us), I think we sometimes reach for that easy stereotype. We *pretend* to be cowboys, individualists, stoics—not necessarily because we believe the stereotype ourselves, but because we hope the grown-ups will buy it. Then, we hope, they'll go away and leave us alone.

It's a teenager's response. Sure, it's slightly immature. But it comes from an aggravation at being condescended to, which I think is often justified.

If the adults would sit and listen, our conversations might get beyond the cowboy stereotypes.

But too often they don't. They just get frustrated—but that leaves *us* with a problem too. As Westerners, we are stuck with the consequences of our pretensions: we have to continually live up to that lonely celluloid image. And, like teenagers, we also have to live with the moments of desperate doubt, when we wonder why it is that we're all alone and not growing up.

Writers on the Range newspaper syndicate, 2004

Part V
FRONTIERS

Wister's versus Turner's Frontier

In the fall my favorite running and hiking routes head east from my home at the base of the mountains, into the plains rather than the peaks. Instead of wilderness, I venture into fenced rangeland, dried grasses, rocky ravines, and meandering dirt roads. Compared to the steep inclines and tall trees, this land has a historical feel, and it gets me thinking about the two greatest proponents of our nation's frontier.

Even the earliest Euro-American settlers defined a boundary of their civilization, but the notion peaked in meaning as that boundary seemed to disappear. In 1893, the historian Frederick Jackson Turner declared that the frontier was closed, since census results no longer showed a line beyond which populations petered out.

Nine years later, Owen Wister published *The Virginian*, a nostalgic view of 1880s Wyoming. The hugely popular novel spawned an entire genre and brought powerful connotations to some of the simple things I see while my feet chug along, such as sagebrush, cattle, and tumbleweed.

As I move through the landscape, I try to reconcile the opposing ways these two men defined the frontier. Turner saw it as a process: people satisfying their urges to explore, exploit, and civilize. Turner fretted that the closing of the frontier could mark a crisis in the American character. But as it played out, he so effectively articulated the notion of frontiering that we have simply applied it to new realms, such as space and technology.

Wister, on the other hand, was uneasy about the process. For him, the frontier was a specific place: the open range. He saw the outdoor life of a

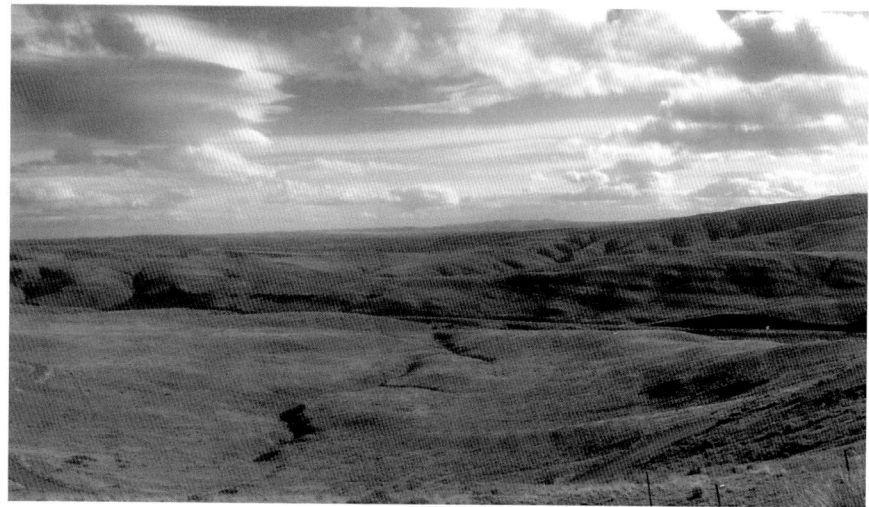

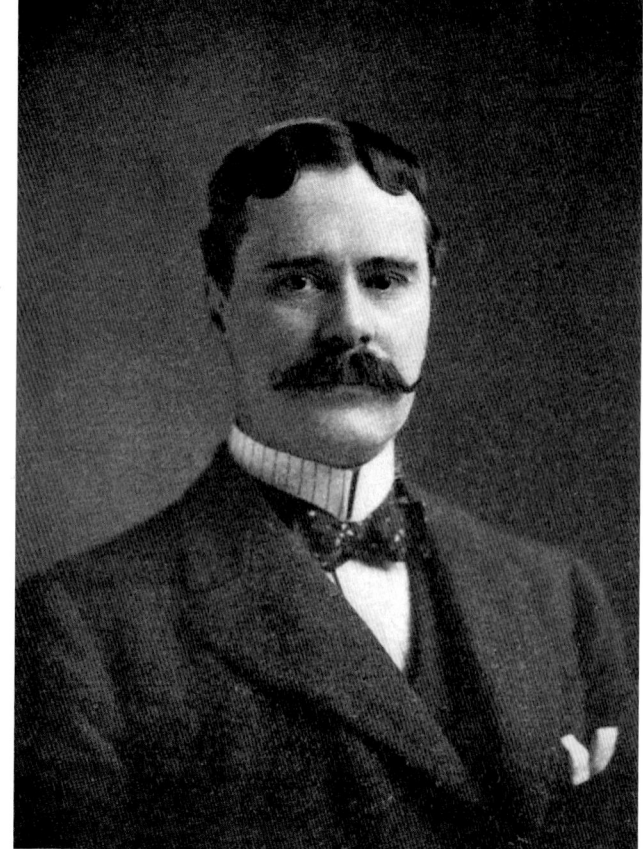

Above: My favorite fall running routes, such as this one north of Bearcreek, take me out into the plains—into what still feels like frontier. *Author photo.*

Right: Owen Wister, a Harvard-educated lawyer, equated the frontier with the open range, and his novel *The Virginian* so vividly captured that glory that Hollywood has used his definition ever since. *Wikimedia photo.*

young, carefree, white male cattle tender as something glorious. He fretted that the march of progress would eliminate it forever. But he so effectively painted his vision of that life that the cattle drive has become a perpetual movie setting and the cowboy hat a never-ending icon.

So both men were deeply right. They articulated a change in turn-of-the-last-century America—and did it so well that those themes have continued their pull on the culture through another hundred-plus years of change.

Such thoughts can get me through my first mile. But as I force my legs to take me farther, I start thinking that both men were actually wrong. Homesteading and prospecting booms continued, especially in Montana, for twenty-five years after Turner's proclamation. And as author Dayton Duncan noted in *Miles from Nowhere*, by 1990, America had more counties meeting the Census Bureau's 1890 definition of "frontier" (a population density of fewer than two people per square mile) than it did in Turner's day.

Meanwhile, despite Wister's claims, the open-range era ended not because of the arrival of civilizing women, population growth, or even the invention of barbed wire. It just wasn't economically viable, as Terry Jordan showed in his book *North American Cattle Ranching Frontiers*.

But when Wister the novelist gave a narrative form to Turner's thesis—the frontier was closed because that open range was fenced and those young men and cattle now less than free—the two men's ideas merged in public minds, validating each other. Wister and Turner marched hand-in-hand through the twentieth century.

Over the last decade or two, frontier notions have come under fire. Critics have observed that Turner's concept of empty land ignores and thus oppresses Indians and Hispanos. His assumption that resources existed for us to exploit has contributed to today's environmental problems. Meanwhile, Wister's critics have pointed out that valorizing white male macho cowboys similarly clashes with the value today's society places on diversity.

As my route reaches its homestretch, however, I often get a bit nostalgic. I dread leaving this unpeopled landscape, getting back in my car, and returning to my civilized town life. A landscape of grass and fence—even more than one of forests and cliffs—offers a sense of possibility. This is a place where not just wildlife but civilizations could live. This is a place where I could re-start my life, for whatever reason I wanted. This is a place just like town, except it's not (yet) town.

This is the ragged edge of urban civilization, and like Turner and Wister, I wish it could be here forever.

2005

Disney's New Western Frontier

The Walt Disney Company is coming to Yellowstone National Park, and the typical level of response is to joke that maybe its signature mouse will become "Mickey Moose." That's too bad, because this new venture by a savvy multinational corporation mirrors the development of the West's previous frontiers.

In a quiet 2005 announcement, Disney said it intended to test-launch a "Quest for the West" weeklong vacation tour of Yellowstone, Grand Teton, and the Jackson Hole area. Wyoming and Hawaii are the first two destinations for "Adventures by Disney," a vacation concept marketed to people who already take Disney vacations such as cruises.

Disney thus tests the waters of ecotourism (nature-oriented tourism that seeks to minimize environmental impacts). It's an economic frontier: a new, unorganized market, much like furs in the 1830s or the Internet in the 1990s. Some pioneers have proved its viability, and now a large corporation is moving in.

That's the way frontiers always work: adventurers explore a new area, and then someone with more money and organization comes in to control it. The discovery of California gold led to a rush of forty-niners, but by the 1880s, most Western mining activity was run by large corporations. Early Western farmers built small irrigation schemes, but after 1900, most dams were huge, complicated projects built by the federal government. A computer hacker might start a company in his garage, but venture capitalists later organize and fund it to succeed.

Frontiers thus always attract two types of people, romantics and capitalists. Romantics love the adventure: panning for gold, cowboying on a cattle drive, landing on the moon. Capitalists love the opportunity to make money by organizing and controlling a new arena.

So far ecotourism has attracted lots of romantics: people who love nature, want to preserve it, and are excited about the possibility of eradicating the alleged "jobs versus the environment" gap. Small, local, well-informed outfitters across the West have shared their passion and knowledge with a select clientele.

Disney, on the other hand, excels at organization and control. Most amusement parks were small and local until Disneyland and Disney World made them global juggernauts. More recently, Disney capitalized the New Urbanism architectural trend to create a phenomenally successful real estate development called Celebration, Florida. So I wouldn't be surprised if Disney also succeeded with its version of ecotourism.

That's good for Disney. But is it good for society or the environment?

The promise of ecotourism is that it marshals market forces behind environmental causes. A Disney-in-Yellowstone requires a vibrant Yellowstone, and so we could potentially foresee a day when Disney's powerful lobbyists call for strengthened endangered species laws to protect the grizzlies and wolves that contribute to its bottom line. (What if Disney ran tours in the Arctic National Wildlife Refuge, thus adding its voice in opposition to drilling there?)

On the other hand, the danger of unfettered capitalism is that private profits can come at the expense of public resources. Indeed, capitalist activity on previous frontiers has led to many of our current environmental problems. Many grasslands still haven't recovered from overgrazing by huge corporate cattle ranches in the late nineteenth century. Likewise, individual gold-panners could sometimes make a mess, but it takes an organized corporate body to make a Superfund site.

Some previous pioneers even soiled their own beds. Once organized into efficient companies, fur trappers nearly exterminated the beaver they depended on. Timber companies in the late nineteenth century so overcut their private lands in the upper Midwest that Gifford Pinchot organized federal forest preserves to save them from their own greed.

Could the same sort of fate befall ecotourism? In some places, I can picture new hotels, roads, and other infrastructure crowding out the very wildlife habitat that created the need for them. I can picture each corporation saying the problem is not *its* hotel but everybody else's. I can picture this not because corporations are inherently bad, but because that's the only way for them to compete.

The lesson we claim to have learned from the abuses of capitalism on past frontiers is that when big corporations deal with public goods such as wildlife habitat, they need a countervailing force—government—to speak up for society. But frontiers are, by definition, unexplored territory, which means it's hard to know from a distance what they look like, how they will develop, or which lessons from which previous experiences we need to apply to them.

Writers on the Range newspaper syndicate, 2005

What We Do on Today's Frontier

I went looking for Gary Ferguson in the most remote spot in the continental United States, and I couldn't find him.

Ferguson spent the summer of 2002 in the Thorofare country, just south of the southeast corner of Yellowstone National Park, to write the book *Hawks Rest: A Season in the Remote Heart of Yellowstone*. Some geographer with far too much time on his or her hands had deemed this the one spot in the lower forty-eight farthest from a road. Gary went there with the idea of writing a book that would see what it was like. I went to visit because he was a friend.

At Hawks Rest (the name of a promontory, as well as a Forest Service cabin below it), the valley is broad, the river meandering, the vistas pure. My friends and I followed a well-trodden, surprisingly flat trail about twenty-five miles in from a trailhead east of the Tetons. (That's as far as you can get from a road in twenty-first-century America: twenty-five miles.) We came off Two Ocean Plateau and bogged down in a seemingly endless beaver-generated swamp. In the distance we could admire the smoke of a wildfire so remote it would never be fought. Ah, wilderness.

Then we arrived at Grand Central Station. Hawks Rest may be remote, but that doesn't mean it's empty. In his first seven weeks there, Gary saw more than six hundred people pass through. The day we arrived was no exception.

At the cabin, we met up with Gary's hiking companion LaVoy. We also met the cabin tender from a ranger station twelve miles away, who had ambled over for dinner with the neighbors. Later in the evening we would meet a three-person Forest Service trail crew, using the cabin to tend to their horses and cook mammoth meals. Visiting the following day would be a large party including a Forest Service wilderness supervisor and a biologist. Stopping in one morning would be a dozen college students here to get course credit for repairing fences. And drifting in and out was Kayla Michael, a woman who spends five months every summer in the Thorofare wilderness, on foot, alone. She's been doing it for twenty years.

And that was just at the cabin. A dozen or so camps spread through the valley. We passed several long strings of packhorses. As we ranged over a hundred miles of trail in the area, almost everyone we talked to was headed to or from Hawks Rest. And we were there in August, after the height of fishing season.

The Hawks Rest cabin tender (a volunteer Forest Service position Gary and LaVoy had taken) always ends up hosting a party. But Gary had come to Hawks Rest to write a book. He needed somewhere more remote than the most remote spot in the country. So he set up a backpacking tent just west of the cabin, to hide. That's where I eventually found him.

Because of these experiences, Gary's book is not exactly the one he intended to write—about wilderness and ecology and the status of the elk herds and grizzly bears in this stunning stretch of mountain country. Instead he writes about all the people he met and all the crazy things they're doing. There's Kayla Michael, who post-holes through early June snow with what must be at least an eighty-pound pack of her summer's gear. There's Yellowstone park ranger Bob Jackson, on an epic crusade against poachers. There are all sorts of horse-packers, mostly from Utah, where they've seen cable TV shows playing up the fishing here.

And then there are the outfitters. They carry guns. They get in feuds. They complain about the government. One guide leaves a client who's been injured by a falling horse on the side of the trail with just a fleece jacket and a water bottle. (No sleeping bag, no matches, no pepper spray.) The guide, shepherding six people who'd each paid $250 a day, had neither a radio nor a partner, and left the injured man so as to race ahead to Hawks Rest in hopes Gary and LaVoy could help.

Gary tries to write an evenhanded book, but he's documented too many stories like that one. An outfitter puts cowbells on each of his thirty-five head of stock at night, forcing nearby campers to move out of "his territory." An outfitter poaches a mountain lion inside Yellowstone and hangs a sign in his camp bragging, "—— gets pussy." Outfitters and their crews quarrel in a trailhead parking lot, hands on their holsters ready to draw.

As a portrait of the last wilderness, *Hawks Rest* ends up being more a portrait of the romantic last frontier. It looks a lot like the frontier of the 1880s, with the difference that our perception of the frontier of the 1880s is largely make-believe, a product of Zane Grey's imagination.

Why do you carry a handgun in the Thorofare? Because of the bears, everyone says. But nobody carries pepper spray, and nobody carries the gun in a saddlebag or a back pocket. Everybody wears hip holsters, just like their favorite movie cowboys.

Why do you hire an outfitter? To make your backcountry trip easier, everyone says. But many outfitters just preen and primp, making colorful, movie-quality cowboy utterances but otherwise treating their customers like dog crap. (It's not all of them, as Gary bends over backward to point out. And many of the customers are drunks and fools who perhaps deserve to be treated like dog crap. But still, aren't they the ones who are paying the $250 a day?)

Why do you go to the Thorofare wilderness? To get away from it all, everyone says. But nobody goes to the adjacent empty valleys. Nobody goes to places they haven't seen on TV. Everybody congregates at Hawks Rest, a place that feels like civilization.

It would be nice to dismiss the book as a curmudgeonly complaint by a nature writer who didn't get his solitude. But visiting Hawks Rest, I was struck by the same things Gary was. To hell with the nature—the people made this a very American place, an important slice of mountain culture that's too rarely examined.

And sure, it would be easy to dismiss those people as a bunch of yayhoos and jackasses. Except that I did a version of the same thing. I went to Hawks Rest not for its wilderness but because Gary was there. I went with five buddies, including one who has horses so we could bring lots of stuff. I wore a bandana around my head because I thought it made me look cool. (I got the pictures back. It didn't.) When I decided to be prepared for any bear encounter by practicing pulling my pepper spray out of its holster, I remember that holster being suspiciously close to my hip. And I remember giving the motion just a hint of swagger: a kid practicing his draw.

Hawks Rest ends up being a story about all of us. Why do we love wilderness? Maybe it's not the scenery or the wildlife or the physical challenge or the serenity or all the other noble things we like to tell ourselves. Maybe the mountains just give us room to act out whatever silly fantasies we developed back in civilization. We want to make fools of ourselves, kids in a giant sandbox we call nature.

2003

Part VI
THE NEW WEST

All-Harley Cowboys

Once upon a time, I'm sure, the arrival of hundreds of bikers in your town was intimidating. By 1998, it was somewhat comical, as bald, beer-bellied men creaked off their motorcycles and wallowed around in leather sweatpants. These were not thugs. They were a walking definition of "mid-life crisis."

At first I didn't know what to make of their gathering, called "The Iron Horse Rodeo: An All-Harley Event." Then I decided that it was the ultimate "New West" weekend.

The centerpiece was literally a biker rodeo, with games of skill: going fast or slow, around obstacles or grabbing things from the air. There was also a Poker Run through the surrounding mountain landscape, a wet T-shirt contest, and a street dance featuring (of all things) a reggae band.

Several waitresses commented on how polite and generous the bikers were. Good tippers. Given the price of a new Harley Davidson, that shouldn't have been surprising: most of them had funds to spare. So the throttle of their engines sounded to many local merchants like money.

With downtown parking spaces marked off "for motorcycles only," and with the fully costumed drivers of those bikes wandering everywhere and congregating on every corner, our town was transformed into a movie set for an alien planet. And yet, when you looked closer, the sight had familiar trappings. It was the Old West reincarnated. The bikers wore enough metal and leather to make you wonder how mining and ranching could be considered declining industries. And the infuriating whine of their motors reminded me of a chainsaw, although without the subsequent, satisfying *thwap* of tree against earth.

The annual weekend's original organizers, I'm sure, got a kick out of reinventing the rodeo as a biker event. As it grew, they may have also appreciated the irony of what used to be "outlaw bikers" now being welcomed as "economic development." But it didn't strike me until 1998—when the name was changed from the "All-Harley Rodeo"—how deep were the organizers' mythological ambitions. I mean, "Iron Horse"…didn't that used to be the railroad?

It made me realize how empty our old myths are: savvy marketers can portray bikes as both horses *and* trains; can portray their riders as both cowpokes *and* outlaws.

That year, many people in the media were talking about an incipient, triumphant transformation of the region's economy and culture away from its cowboy-hatted, frontier-influenced past. But my view was more cynical. To me this was the New West: take a myth, an image; twist it around to fit your product; and make a lot of money.

It wasn't just bikers. Everyone was claiming the cowboy legacy: telecommuters, miners, movie stars…How are yuppies tied to their computers, wage slaves running machines in underground tunnels, and insecure millionaires who tote around their personal espresso machines similar to people who herd cattle from horseback? That's irrelevant. The point is, they want to believe it, and you can make money by pretending to agree with them.

People interested in environmental politics mistakenly believed that the New West was about their issues. But I didn't hear any of the Harley riders talking about the demise of extractive-based industries or the expansion of telecommunications infrastructure or incentives for habitat protection on private lands. Mostly they talked about…their bikes.

Because *that* was the New West: simply a place where you could buy whatever image you'd always dreamed about or seen on a big screen. Whether you wanted to be an "outlaw biker" or a "carefree retiree" or a "rock climber," the first and most important step was to buy a T-shirt.

Luxury log cabins. Exclusive hunting preserves. Fur-trapper rendezvous reenactments. Helicopter skiing. All of them took nineteenth-century myths of open, rugged lands, dressed them up with current amenities, and sold the image.

Thinking about all this started getting me pretty depressed. But then, as an East Coast refugee myself, I realized the flip-side: at least the West still has myths to misappropriate. Let's face it: Harleys invading Connecticut just wouldn't have much to do.

The funny thing was, despite the awful noise and the stench of burned rubber, despite the bikers' apparent sexism, their ridiculous get-ups, and their confused reinterpretations of history, I *liked* many of them as individuals. And this, I decided, was why. In a society where we suffer from an excess of luxury and a dearth of ways to put it in wider perspective, the all-Harley rodeo participants embodied a West that is still the sort of place where we see life in terms of myths.

Writers on the Range newspaper syndicate, 1998

The "New West" Is an Old Concept

I just finished reading a novel called *Old West—And New*. It's got the "New West" down pat: onerous federal regulations; land increasingly carved into tiny patches of weeds; rich, clueless outsiders moving in and ruining things; politicians stealing elections with underhanded last-minute charges; lives devastated by illegal narcotics; and a homogeneity of development in which new towns look like anyplace else, "exchanging the picturesque for the commonplace."

Funny thing is, the book was published in 1933.

As we enter a new century, we're constantly throwing around the phrase "New West." On Amazon.com, for example, fifty-nine books feature the phrase in their titles. And this is at least the tenth essay in the "Writers on the Range" series with a lead featuring the phrase. The past ones have covered everything from trailer trash to wildlife.

Introducing the 1997 book *Atlas of the New West*, William Riebsame wrote, "Traditional life ways—logging, mining, drilling, farming, and ranching—contrast sharply with the new economy of services and information, ostentatious wealth, and tourism." This is as close to a definition as I've found for the notoriously vague notion. But I used to agree: these contrasts—sheep versus services; oil versus microbrew; "logged out" versus "logged on"—represented the New West. This novel has changed my mind. It paints similar contrasts over sixty years previously, before the technology revolution that supposedly created the new ways.

In the novel, the onerous federal regulation was Prohibition, not environmental policies. The weedy parcels resulted from dry farming, not residential suburbs. The invading hordes were Midwestern shopkeepers, not Californian day-traders.

But if the issues differed ever so slightly, the attitudes perfectly matched today's. The "true Westerners" were independent spirits who distrusted government, loved seeing livestock in wide-open spaces, and preferred ornery characters to idealistic community-builders.

So the "New West" embodies a storyline that never changes: The "old" and "true" always fight against the "new," moneyed, and somehow false. Progress and conformity have ruined everywhere else; the West is the last chance to make things right. Which means that change is always bad. It makes me wonder if trappers referred to the first cowboys as the "New West."

In the late 1800s, the term "New South" arose as a label for the former slave states. Vaguely post-racial, the "New South" usually referred to a land of railroads and textile mills run by progressive businesspeople, though the term was slapped on almost any development that represented something other than the plantation.

"New South" boosters painted their land as rich, just, and triumphant, writes Wayne Mixon in the *Encyclopedia of Southern Culture*—and it was almost all a lie. African Americans were still little better than slaves, Northerners controlled the industries, and most Southerners were still poor farmers. The illusory image inspired such hope that the phrase endured for more than a hundred years. But during that time it allowed Southerners to become resignedly complacent about social ills, environmental abuses, and the rise of a mass culture to replace unique regional traditions.

Does the term "New West" do the same thing? It strikes me that we throw it at anything that's not cowboys. We have tied up a bundle of values, industries, and attitudes and labeled them all the "Old West." Too often, the few Westerners who do embrace change see this Old West as the root of all problems. Thus, everything labeled "New West" they anoint as progressive, rich, just, and triumphant.

But the cowboy at the heart of the Old West is rarely an actual cattle tender, more an invention of novelists. Philadelphian Owen Wister penned *The Virginian* in 1902 to mourn the passage of a romanticized (perhaps wholly invented) heroic figure. Along with a slew of protégés and imitators, he thus established the Old West as something both unique and finished.

One of Wister's followers was Caroline Lockhart, who wrote a half dozen Westerns between 1911 and 1921. Then, after a dozen years in other pursuits, she wrote a final novel that tried to follow her imagined cowboy heroes into anticlimactic latter-day lives. They became tourism promoters and barbers and gas station owners. But the only important thing in their lives—for the characters themselves, as well as the author who created them—was that they used to have these mythic cowboy lives and didn't anymore. This is the book I just read, the one her publisher called *Old West—And New*.

Writers on the Range newspaper syndicate, 2000

Ten Years and Counting on a Meaningless Phrase

The summer of 2006 marked a tenth anniversary for me: the first time I used the phrase "New West" in a published essay. And the anniversary marked the point when I had to admit that I had absolutely no idea what the term means.

Back in 1996, I was writing about the Unabomber and the Montana Freemen. I proposed that their misanthropy and misguided individualism were "the last gasp of tired frontier notions" and that "if we are to build a 'new West,' a culture to lead this country into the 21st century, I believe we must base it on concepts of tolerance and community."

I still sort of like the sentiment, though I must admit it sounds like a third-rate Bill Clinton impersonator. (Since the rest of the essay is no better, it's not included in this collection.) Furthermore, the quotes I put around the phrase New West suggest that I was caught up in a linguistic fad, that I'd heard the phrase and wanted to put in my two cents about what it meant.

As I recall, the fad embodied a hope that the rural West was indeed going to become a more community-minded, tolerant, environmentally friendly, and dare-I-say liberal place. These changes were going to come about through waves of immigration, technological improvements, tourism, and understanding.

Did they? In politics, change has been slow at best, with the Rocky Mountains generally placed in the "red state" category. Indeed, continuing discussions of a Red/Blue divide bear an eerie similarity to those old Old/New West discussions. Tolerance, community, environment: the cultural fault line still exists—and generalizations still place the West on its non-liberal side.

Meanwhile, has tourism proved a more sustainable approach to Western resources than logging, mining, or ranching? Well, sometimes. The best ecotourism does indeed use a low-impact, high-education "take only pictures" approach—while the worst tourism trashes wildlife habitat with sprawling hotels and mini-malls. In other words, tourism is a resource-dependent economic sector that can be small and sustainable or can be industrial and hideous—which is also the case for logging and ranching. In this sense the West's economic structure is hardly new.

Nevertheless, the phrase New West gets applied all over the place. A 2006 Google search yields 3.75 million results, the top ten of which include an upscale rustic furniture manufacturer, a Montana-based health insurer, an online newsmagazine featuring articles about Missoula wildfires and Boise coffeeshops, and a wholesaler of bison and ostrich meat.

Many people still define the New West by similar examples: a ski town microbrewery, a Lycra-clad mountain biker, or a software company with a mountain view.

Yet aren't these things—microbreweries, mountain bikes, software, espresso, and ostrich meat—merely the fads of the 1990s? The fads have passed, into obscurity or ordinariness. What's more, they were never particularly Western. Sure, it was odd to see them dressed in cowboy trappings. But was it any odder than such trappings on 1940s motels, 1950s lunchboxes, or 1980s missile silos?

Without a doubt, the region has experienced a great deal of change in the last ten or fifteen years. But then again, so has most of the world. So what's New about this West? Is it that the pace of change has quickened, that the West is more closely linked to such global trends?

In this view, the New West refers to the region's increasing ties to a globalizing economy. Yet this definition doesn't recall just the 1990s—it recalls the entire Euro-American history of the West. Surely nineteenth-century Native Americans faced increasing ties to a globalized economy. Indeed, that's the explanation we cling to when we want to minimize the evil racism behind their tragic fate. And, on a lesser scale, that's the explanation we provide for the passing of everything from the fur-trading era to the open range.

"Increasing ties to a globalized economy" is not a bad theory, as theories go—it has a fair bit of explanatory power. But new? Hardly. Indeed, that which we are tempted to call New about the West is actually what's most enduring.

2006

Part VII
AUTHENTICITY

A Permanent State of Not-Quite-Decay

The allure of a ghost town is its state of decay. Bereft of people, furnishings, and other signs of residence, it gives us room to project ourselves into those empty spaces. If the buildings are not just run down but formerly elegant—with decorative trim on the leaning timbers or a grand staircase under the gaps in the roof—we're apt to be even happier. Now we can project ourselves into another era's dreams.

When I stumbled across the Caroline Lockhart homestead in 2000, it was in part this ghost town–ness that attracted me. In this old ranch complex on the east slopes of the Pryor Mountains, a friend and I pushed open creaky doors and walked gingerly over sloping floorboards. We marveled at not only the valley scenery and romantic setting; not only the lonely abandonment of the dozen-plus log buildings on the empty site; not only the absence of telephone, television, or indoor plumbing. We marveled at this window into a passed glory, the ease by which we could imagine Lockhart living out her cowboy fantasies in this incredibly remote spot from 1925 to 1951.

I spent the next seven years enriching that projection by writing Lockhart's biography. I combed through old diaries, newspapers, and novels, trying to bring Lockhart back to life in some small way. Meanwhile, the ranch buildings themselves went on a similar journey.

"The National Park Service used to have a 'decompose naturally' philosophy," says Chris Finley, an archaeologist and historic restoration specialist at the Bighorn Canyon National Recreation Area, which now

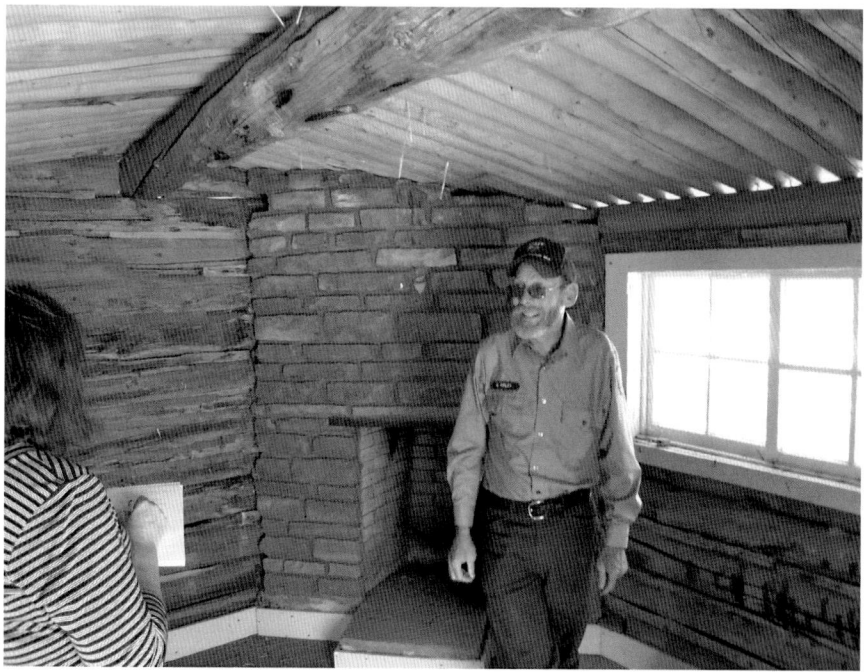

Chris Finley, shown here in a restored guest cabin on the Caroline Lockhart ranch in 2007, has sought to restore old buildings like these while maintaining their rustic authenticity. *Author photo.*

owns the Lockhart ranch. "They'd let an old ranch fall apart, and then once it became a safety hazard, they'd burn it."

That policy, however, meant the loss of great cultural resources. For example, at Bighorn Canyon, the Lockhart ranch provides a fascinating window into Montana's early homesteading and cattle-ranching eras. The same can also be said of the neighboring Ewing/Snell ranch and ghost town of Hillsboro.

The Park Service later adopted a policy of stabilization and repair, Finley says, and more recently has chosen to give such resources new life through restoration.

Restoring the Lockhart ranch, or any such historic property, involves a delicate balance. If they were still inhabited, each building would eventually come to a crossroads: does it get modernized or destroyed? Finley instead tries to keep the buildings in a permanent state of not-quite-decay, thus providing a permanent, authentic view of life in the past.

The most glamorous work happens in the summertime, when crews of students—from Minnesota State University, Northwest (Wyoming) College,

AUTHENTICITY

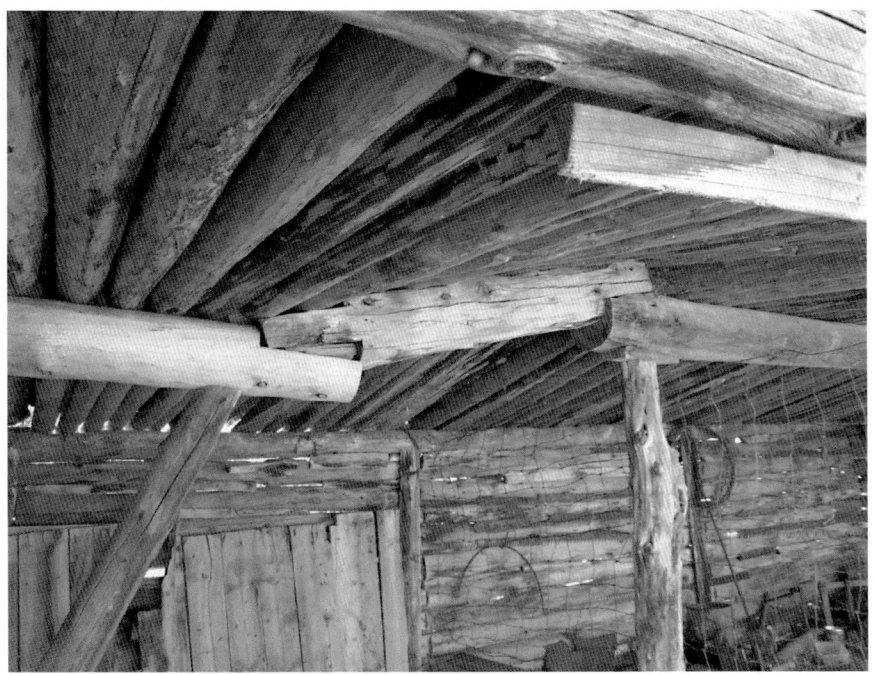

In an outbuilding on the Caroline Lockhart ranch, the original builders used a shortcut to link two wayward ridgepoles—so what should a restorer do? *Author photo.*

and anywhere else Finley can round them up—mimic the brutal physical labor of the old-time carpenters.

"I had the Montana Conservation Corps in here last summer splitting poles like Abraham Lincoln," Finley says. "Now we'll have to figure out how to blacken them" to match the aged timbers they will complement. Much of their work comes in simply trying to stop nature from reclaiming what humans have abandoned. Standing in front of the post office in Hillsboro, Finley says, "I knew these buildings weren't built into the hillside. The hill moved in on them." So one summer the Conservation Corps shoveled eleven feet of dirt away from the building's back side.

The results are not always obvious to the untutored eye. A bizarre diagonal tries to link two wayward ridgepoles—was it a builder's shortcut or a restoration crew making an exact replication of that shortcut? An old blacksmith shop appears full of junk—is it junk the smith once worked on or did Finley collect it from around the ranch? An outhouse features a seat consisting of two planks—is it a museum piece or a functioning privy?

That last paradox has fooled even Finley. "We've had to put Plexiglas over the seat since there's no hole under it," he says. "I was amazed at how people will always use an outhouse, even one that's clearly under construction with tools lying all over the place."

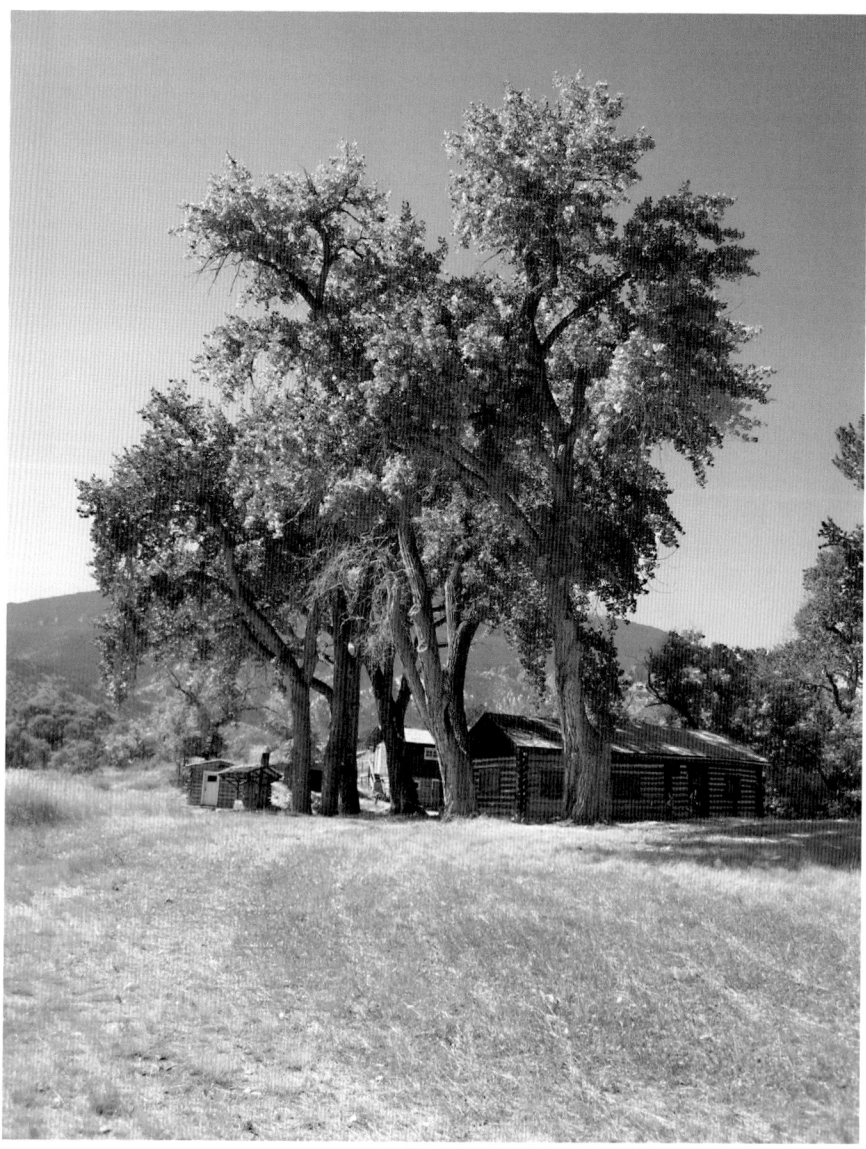

The majestic cottonwoods at the Caroline Lockhart ranch, shown here in 2007, had to be cut down in 2010 because old, falling limbs threatened historic structures. But because Chris Finley had taken cuttings, their replacements are exact replicas. *Author photo.*

Yet re-creating these historic features also involves a good deal of research and analysis. For example, old photographs can show how a ridgepole stuck out from the side of a building or what types of apple, pear, and peach trees composed an old orchard. Finley discovers old paint colors by taking off moldings and nurtures seedlings for the time when they will have to replace a dying cottonwood.

Along the way, the research also provides delicious evidence of how characters of the past dealt with hardships. For example, Lockhart had an old-style plank floor in her kitchen. She liked the look of it, but mice could easily creep through its gaps. So she kept two bullsnakes in the house to kill the mice. Today, by contrast, the Park Service uses gravel fill beneath the planks to keep out the rodents.

Such applications of current-day technology to simulate old environments lead to some of the biggest debates that Finley has with himself, his team, and other preservationists. Do you add drip flashing to a roof? It's not historically authentic, but it extends the life of a restoration by at least ten years. Do you add French drains to pull water away from delicate log construction? Again, the technique was not available when the buildings were constructed in the first half of the twentieth century, but 99 percent of the public may never notice it. Do you chink a log structure with a modern imitation-mud chink? Real mud would be more historic but would require much more maintenance and hasten structural decay.

Finley even spends weekends going to garage sales and coordinating with a network of folks on the lookout for vintage materials. "Lockhart had a wind generator powering a battery that she used to run a Zenith radio," he says. "She paid fifteen dollars for it new; I found one in a dump." On another occasion he bought and dismantled a 1905 schoolhouse near Lovell, Wyoming, because its battered siding matched the Hillsboro properties he was restoring. "When you start talking to people about what you want to do with their stuff, they're willing to help," he says.

Indeed, he's developed quite a team. "One of my students is a stonemason," he boasts. "I have a blacksmith who re-creates historic hardware. An exhibit specialist, a former bush pilot from Alaska, two local schoolteachers, and a fellow who gives me two months every year repairing and replicating historic doors and windows."

It's a form of creative salvage—re-creating historic environments from whatever is at hand. In that sense, it resembles the way these remote environments were created in the first place. And it seems to be a particular point of pride for Finley, who himself grew up in a similar region, the Book Cliffs country of Colorado, in the 1940s and '50s.

While most of us spend mere hours in a ghost town, projecting ourselves into utterly foreign environments, Finley is full-time reanimator of a history not far removed from his own childhood.

"I like to think of it as 'cowboy craftsmanship,'" he says. "Today we might say it's lacking, but it's pretty neat to see how they made do."

Montana Magazine, 2008

Vacation to the 1830s

Amid the cottonwoods and aspens, the hot sun and gentle breeze of a Rocky Mountain summer, an afternoon at a "mountain man rendezvous" glides by with the sort of leisure that spawns striking ideas. Here are two: First, the young boys who used to play Cowboys and Indians have adopted a somewhat more politically correct era for their pretending. Second, they're no longer all boys.

In the 1830s, trappers and traders in the northern Rockies would gather each summer to send their furs eastward and spend their pay at a weekslong party and trade show. A modern-day rendezvous reenacts such a camp. Dozens of them are held each summer throughout the West, often in locations that did not host the original gatherings.

At one I visited in 2001 near Red Lodge, tipis and wall tents were strewn through a half-acre meadow and the surrounding trees. Though the site was just a quarter mile from the highway, the trees blocked most views of twenty-first-century life. From certain angles, I could see an old grain elevator, a modern home, or the camp's makeshift parking lot. But most of the angles supported the illusion of time travel.

Rendezvousers dress in hand-sewn shirts, trousers, or dresses of cotton, wool, or tanned hides. Many of the men wear beards; most have graying hair (often ponytailed and/or balding). Beneath the costumes, many look like unreconstructed hippies, and it's tempting to label the rendezvous a weird remnant of the '60s.

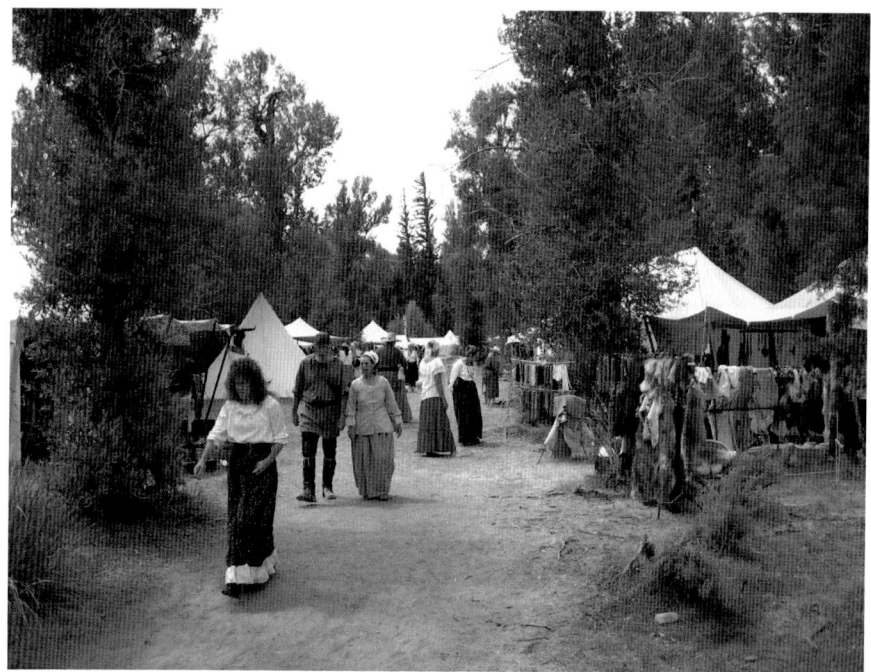

At rendezvous encampments, such as this one at the Rocky Mountain National Rendezvous at Henry's Fork (near Green River, Wyoming) in 2008, everyone dresses in period costume. *Courtesy Tressa Fahrenthold.*

But it's clearly much more than that. I saw no naked stoners lying listlessly along the creek. I did see dozens of participants explaining in considerable detail various aspects of life here 160 years ago. To be accepted in rendezvous culture requires no small amount of work, and participants are clearly here because they love this slice of history.

For today's historical romantics, the fur-trading era is more appropriate than the eras of cowboys-and-cattlemen or the Indian Wars. "The country was brand-new and being discovered," participant Jean Busch told me. "It hadn't been changed to man's needs." Rendezvousers see mountain men as living in relative harmony with the land, one another, and Native Americans.

Most of the activity at a modern rendezvous focuses on tools and toys: black-powder rifles, axes, knives, hides, and hard apple cider. Participants delight in duplicating mountain-man accents ("git," "rilly") and lingo (calling the camp boss a "booshway"). But there's also an underlying philosophy: As today's society increasingly values a pristine environment rather than one reshaped by man, and multicultural cooperation rather than the manifest destiny of white male individualism, historical reenactments follow suit.

Some rendezvous also function as tourist attractions. This one advertised its free RV parking and charged three dollars admission for "good clean family fun." Of course, in the tourist industry these days, that translates as "shopping." Several establishments offered for sale reproductions of 1830s wares—especially the clothing, tents, and other accouterments of reenactment.

The tourism/retail component generates revenue that helps the camp pay for safe drinking water and other infrastructure required in a land that has been changed to meet man's needs. It also provides a way for those hooked on this scene—who possess some of the most knowledge and character in camp—to make a living running the circuit all summer.

IT ALSO, HOWEVER, leads to conflicts between authenticity and profit. For example, the hand-lettered, old-timey signs reading "Master Card and Visa Accepted" detract somewhat from the historical illusion. Worse, unregulated vendors may attempt to sell profitable wares from other eras. At Red Lodge, according to an official program, the rendezvous organizers "allow representation of a broader time period," including something called "the Gunfighter era of the Old West."

Historical purists fume. Occasional participant Jerry Fahrenthold, a fur-trade history buff, said that only 10 to 15 percent of such a commercial-style rendezvous is correct. "Few, if any mountaineers—the term used in the old days—had beards, and none were fat with beer bellies. Indian women did not like beards. [Nobody wore] dead animals on their heads.

"Events east of the Mississippi are far more historically accurate," Fahrenthold says. Although some closed-to-the-public Western events achieve similar aims, he attributes the inaccuracies to Western individualism, people wanting to do it their own way. Thus, as rendezvous organizers argue these points, they often arrive at the all-too-familiar issue of how much power should be granted a central authority (in this case, the "booshway") to define community standards, the appropriate uses of community-governed land, and even the set of agreed-upon facts on which to base these debates.

On the other hand, Fahrenthold said, "Civil War reenactments revive old animosities and glorify a horrible, wasteful war. Rendezvous reenactments represent an escape from Western greed and a quest for the simpler, less stressful, more idyllic Indian way of life. They can also show the exploitation and the harm it did."

White women did not participate in 1830s rendezvous. But today women make up almost half the reenactment participants, and it's not always obvious that their dress is Native American. I found their presence surprising. Not only the tradition (akin to a hunting camp) but also most of the toys struck me as bastions of a male world. But in separate conversations, Busch and participant Kerri Boggio gave similar reasons for attending.

"These are the friendliest people you'll ever run into," Boggio said. "When we bring our kids, we don't have to worry about them" because everyone in camp will watch over them.

Kids seem to enjoy this slow life, far from malls and video games. Again, I expressed surprise. But Busch, whose children are now grown, said, "When I brought my kids here, it used to take two weeks for me to get shoes back on them afterward." They loved being out from under parents' watchful eyes, barefoot and free.

Busch, too, remarked that rendezvousers tend to be "kid-friendly—gentle and kind." While she enjoys beads and clothes of natural fibers—cotton and wool rather than rayon and polyester—Busch is clearly attracted to the event chiefly by the people and the way they interact.

"It's like neighborhoods used to be, when I was a kid," she said. "I miss that era."

For a country so supposedly ignorant of history, America is full of reenactments: colonial villages, Civil War battles, restored Victorian homes. As a nation, we often place our virtues and strengths in bygone times. In this sense, I found Busch's comment particularly telling: a mountain-man rendezvous' biggest accomplishment is that these hippie-looking folks shooting antique guns and sleeping in tipis are in large part seeking to reenact the Ozzie-and-Harriet 1950s.

Unfortunately, the historical record shows that mountaineers were pretty hard on nature—not as bad as modern society, with its plastic waste that never degrades, but incrementally worse than a nomadic Indian camp. Though they saw themselves as freely coexisting with the glorious environment, trappers were steeped in Euro-American ideals of conquest, exploitation, and waste. Though they saw a West of unbounded plenty, the mountaineers were the initial agents of their Eden's destruction. Their explorations paved the way for subsequent waves of settlers, each of whom further despoiled the pristine landscape the mountaineers so loved.

And so by the end of my visit to the 1830s, I found the authenticity bittersweet. I admired the reenactors' knowledge and commitment; I liked their enthusiasm for antiques and reproductions, their quest for a simpler life. I envied their passion. But I decided that I personally would find it depressing to reenact this time period. It's as if, portraying Adam and Eve, the mountain-man rendezvous captures the moment *after* biting the apple: the act of sewing fig leaves into aprons. That may well be an interesting craft, but to me its existence speaks, through the ages, of something far too troubling about humankind.

2001

Clarence Mulford's Odd Western Journey

A 2006 short-story collection, *The Greatest Cowboy Stories Ever Told*, reprinted a long-forgotten 1911 short story by Clarence E. Mulford. I'm glad that Mulford is getting the attention, because the creator of Hopalong Cassidy is one of my favorite Western heroes—though not for any of the reasons you might think.

I was not yet born during the Hoppymania of the early 1950s. I have no Hopalong lunchbox, cereal bowl, or bedspread. I saw my first Hopalong movie at age forty-one—and I found it quite dreadful.

Actually, Clarence Mulford found the movies (and most of the TV shows, which were simply edited versions of the movies) dreadful as well. In the movies, William Boyd played Hopalong as the good-humored, even-tempered, well-scrubbed, trustworthy uncle you always wished you had. Boyd's Hopalong is a teetotaling middle-aged do-gooder, dressed all in black, with the belt of his clean and well-creased slacks riding high across his waist.

That's the exact opposite of Mulford's Hopalong Cassidy, a tough, unpolished, redheaded twenty-three-year-old who drank, swore, gambled, spit tobacco, and mercilessly if good-naturedly teased his fellow cowboys. Mulford got rich off Hollywood's transformation of his fictional character, but he was never happy about it.

Oddly, however, as far as I can tell, William Boyd actually was a great improvement. Mulford's novels were ludicrous pulp, with lines—like "Shorty reached for his revolver and yelled, 'Yore a liar!'"—that must have been trite even when he started writing back in 1905. His plots were absurd, his characters flat, his structuring limp, and his racism and mawkish sentimentality painfully evident. Even Mulford's biographer, Francis M. Nevins, says that Mulford was "intolerably heavy-handed" and a "ponderous stylist" who is "no great pleasure to read."

So why, you may be asking, do I call him a Western hero? Perhaps, you're thinking, even if he didn't write that cowboy life very well, he must have lived it.

Actually, no. Born in Illinois, he did most of his writing in New York City. Once he got rich, he moved to Fryeburg, Maine. He was as opposite a cowboy as you could imagine: he dressed in puttees and plus-fours, and his hobbies included yachting and stamp-collecting.

He spent almost twenty years writing cowboy novels before even setting foot west of the Mississippi River. And when he did, he hated it. He'd grown up reading dime novels and acting them out in the backyard; his writing was an extension of that fantasy. How could reality help but disillusion him?

Yet that inexperience is part of what I admire. Mulford had an encyclopedic knowledge of Western landscape and paraphernalia (literally! learned from encyclopedias!). He kept seventeen thousand cross-indexed file cards, in thirty-four drawers, that he constantly referred to. He insisted on correctness of technical, geographic, and historical details—and wrote so compellingly about them that you felt like you were crossing a certain river with him, even though he'd never been there.

He then married that knowledge to a philosophy that resonated with thousands of cowboy fanatics. He had a gritty sense of self-reliance, a passion for rugged individualism, and a crusty hatred of government. In the late 1930s he stopped writing novels because, he said, he didn't want to pay taxes on whatever they would earn. Later he donated his copyrights to a nonprofit foundation so the government couldn't collect tax revenues off his creations.

Historical accuracy and individual self-reliance were the bedrock for a set of strict, unchanging rules he had for life. He continually used those rules to judge both others and himself.

I myself don't really agree with those rules. I read fiction for character and plot, not historical accuracy. And I think there are times when we can't be self-reliant, when maybe we need an avuncular middle-aged cowboy to come help us out of a jam.

But Mulford insisted that he (not just everyone else) must live by his impossibly strict rules. That's a very Western trait. It's the same trait, I would argue, that we most admire in our favorite Western movie heroes, the John Wayne types. In those movies we call it "honor."

Clarence Mulford may not have composed the world's greatest sentences about honor. But he did live it.

2006

A Regular He-Man Horse

In 1923, a disagreement between East and West almost put a stop to one of the biggest public arts projects in the country. A massive sculpture of the recently deceased William F. "Buffalo Bill" Cody, dreamed up by his namesake Wyoming town, was under construction by New York City's famed society sculptor Gertrude Vanderbilt Whitney.

But when they saw one of Whitney's sketches, folks in Cody didn't like it. Why? The explanation, chronicled in Liza Nicholas's 2007 book *Becoming Western*, isn't what you might think. Codyites might have objected to the way the buckskin-clad figure suggested Wyoming was still some sort of backward wasteland. But they didn't. They might have objected to how little time Whitney had spent in their town or how she'd rejected their proposed site for the memorial. But they didn't. They might have objected to the cost of supplies and services procured in New York, which eventually inflated the project's cost from $50,000 to $250,000. But they didn't. They might have objected to the way Whitney had appropriated their local symbols for her own agenda of value-laden nostalgia. But that wasn't it either.

They objected to the size of Buffalo Bill's horse.

It was too fat, said Caroline Lockhart, editor of the Cody newspaper and chair of the local committee overseeing the memorial, "too much of the polo pony type." She argued that Buffalo Bill would have ridden a more wiry, muscular range horse.

Her fellow Codyites chipped in. The stirrup wasn't big enough, some said, and the feet needed to be bunched closer together rather than thrown

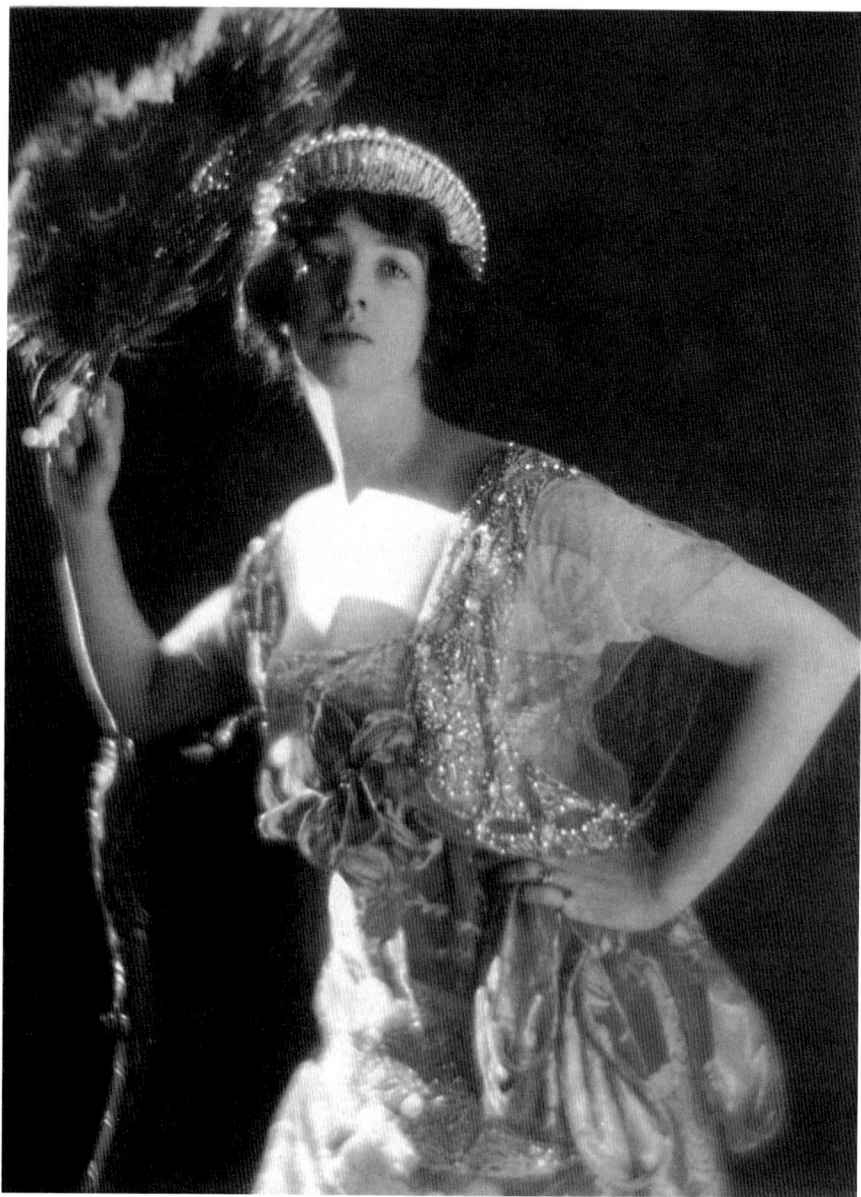

Sculptress Gertrude Vanderbilt Whitney, shown here in society attire in 1916, was a product of wealthy New York. When she decided in 1923 to make a statue of Buffalo Bill Cody, it was part of an effort to redefine him as not merely an entertainer but also a frontier hero. *Library of Congress LC-USZC2-6127.*

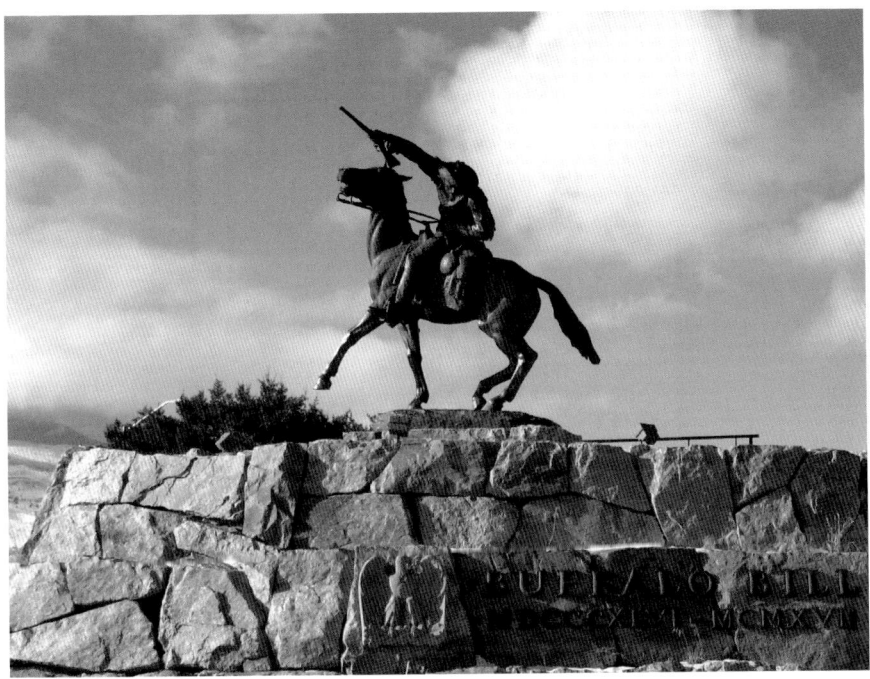

Just north of the Buffalo Bill Historical Center, this 1924 Gertrude Vanderbilt Whitney statue of Buffalo Bill Cody represented Eastern money embracing and co-opting the values of the frontier. But it almost didn't get built because Codyites objected to the authenticity of the horse. *Author photo.*

forward. All in all, summarized local rodeo expert Lloyd Coleman, "It's a society animal—and that won't do for Buffalo Bill. He's got to have a regular he-man horse."

This was a big deal in Cody at the time. In fact, it was so important that Cody leaders shipped to New York a genuine Western horse named Smokey. Smokey was accompanied by Coleman, who rode through Central Park so Whitney could see how Buffalo Bill's horse would have moved.

The first time I encountered this story, it struck me as typifying a Western fascination with trivia. In the big picture, Buffalo Bill had died a pauper, his reputation as an entertainer eclipsed by newer formats such as movies. And Whitney's statue was part of a conscious effort by wealthy Easterners to redefine Buffalo Bill as not merely an entertainer but also a frontier hero, and to label that frontier spirit as uniquely American.

You'd think Wyomingites would have had opinions about this effort. (You'd think they'd have endorsed it, although with ornery Wyomingites one can never be sure.) But they said nothing about the message of the statue, only the details of its presentation.

It would be funny if it weren't so sad, I thought, because the situation was repeated throughout the twentieth century. Upper-class image manipulators from elsewhere redefined the romantic trappings of the cowboy frontier to serve all sorts of incongruous purposes. And Westerners cared only for the authenticity of the details. Cigarette brands, tourist towns, and political careers were built on cowboy-hatted images—but as long as a politician wore his hat properly, it didn't much matter how he voted.

In June 2006, the publisher of *True West* explained a theory of why his magazine's circulation had dropped from the 1960s until he bought it in 1999: "The footnote crowd took over." Overwhelmed with "minutia, like the color of Tom McLaury's hatband at the O.K. Corral gunfight," the magazine failed to provide content that was even aware of any sort of larger message.

Westerners had become so focused on trivia that all they could talk about was footnotes. Some Westerners complain of being colonized by the East, controlled by outside forces, yet when values and history are rewritten, the Western contribution addresses appearances.

As I thought more, however, I lost some of my pessimism. After all, I decided, the footnoting instinct also stands for a quality that makes this region special: practicality. In harsh desert, mountain, and plains environments, people who live in the West have discovered that each tool must be perfectly suited to the situation. Bring the wrong size hat brim, the wrong gas for your stove, or the wrong type of horse, and you'll end up sunburned, hungry, and stranded.

Debating symbolism is something that can be done indoors. But when I venture out into these uniquely gorgeous landscapes—which is the reason I love living here—a neighbor who could deconstruct the symbolism of this event isn't half as valuable as one who will point out errors in my presentation.

2007

Part VIII
HEROES

The Mountain Man Who Outshone His Legends

"Here is our problem," wrote the schoolchildren who called themselves the Committee for the Reburial of Liver-Eating Johnston. "Our class has been to where Johnston is presently buried. It is about 100 yards from the smoggiest, most polluted freeway in Los Angeles."

The burial site didn't seem appropriate, thought these seventh graders back in 1973, for one of the most colorful figures of the famed mountain-man era. John Johnston had cemented his larger-than-life reputation under Montana's Big Sky. Only during the last six weeks of his life, sick and broke, had he journeyed to Southern California, to enter a veterans' hospital. But when he died there in 1900, he was buried in the adjacent cemetery.

Then, seventy-three years after his death, his legend reignited. The Committee for the Reburial of Liver-Eating Johnston wrote of its concerns to various figures throughout the Rockies. It convinced the Veterans' Administration to disinter Johnston's body—but it also set off a feud about what to do with it.

JOHN JOHNSTON WAS born in New Jersey in 1824. As a young man he may have joined a whaling crew or served in the navy during the Mexican War. (Later, he would fight with Union forces in the Civil War.) But sometime in the mid-1840s, he headed west, probably first to western Colorado, and learned how to make his living as a trapper. Trappers roamed throughout the Rockies, collecting pelts of beaver and other animals and gathering every summer for trading and partying at mountain-man "rendezvous" events. As trapping declined in profitability through the mid-1800s, Johnston established a camp at the mouth of Montana's Musselshell River, where he cut wood to sell to steamboats heading up the Missouri.

Johnston stood over six feet tall and weighed at least 220 pounds. He had long arms and huge hands, "as big as a half-bushel of Montana wheat," one contemporary said. He was quick on his feet, a strong fighter with a powerful kick. He wore an enormous beard, and his blue-gray eyes had a merciless depth.

Strangers often found him surly, even paranoid. As the West filled up with other white immigrants, he preferred to make his living off the land. For over fifty years, he trapped, hunted, and chopped wood in various locations, though he especially favored central Montana. On the rare occasions when he spent several months in one place, he might keep a garden and make some friends. But on the whole he preferred the mountains to society.

Mountain men thrived on oral tradition. In boasts and storytelling, their culture emphasized the qualities important to their survival: physical strength, courage, determination, and an ornery sort of generosity exemplified by the way Johnston took care of a suffering Musselshell-area widow nicknamed Crazy Woman. The mountain men also had conflicted attitudes toward Native Americans. Though they frequently admired Indian lifestyles and the courage of Indian warriors, and though many took Indian wives, many also saw Indians as cruel savages and glorified acts of war against them.

Thus, mountain-man legends celebrated victories over both nature and Native Americans. As in other frontier cultures, many of these legends involved a trail of vengeance. A particularly gruesome trail grew up around John Johnston.

According to the legend, soon after moving to Montana Johnston married a Flathead girl, whom he loved so much that he learned her language. But one day when he was out trapping, a Crow war party plundered their cabin and killed his pregnant wife. Johnston swore revenge on the Crows, and exacted it so thoroughly that he became known by the name Crow Killer.

According to another legend, twenty years later, Johnston and some comrades, camped near his old wood yard on the Musselshell, were attacked by a Sioux war party. The mountain men cornered the Sioux in a coulee, and toward the end of the battle, Johnston came across a wounded warrior who shot wildly at him. Running short of rifle cartridges, Johnston pulled out his hunting knife. But as he swung a fatal blow, part of the warrior's flesh—perhaps part of his liver—stuck to Johnston's knife. Returning to his comrades, he told them, "Come on and have a piece! I've ett some, and it's just as good as antelope's liver." When they refused, he lifted the knife to his own mouth. The bright red blood stained his black beard.

That incident gave him a more lasting name: Liver-eating Johnston (often spelled Johnson). Eventually that legend merged with the Crow Killer one, and he was alleged to have eaten the livers of the Crow warriors he'd killed. The legend grew to where he'd killed perhaps three hundred Crows before suddenly forswearing his trail of vengeance. Seeing the Crows' kind treatment of Crazy Woman, he gave up his vendetta and by the 1870s became a great friend to his former enemies.

One of the amazing features of the history of the American West is how its oral traditions so thoroughly entered national consciousness. Hearing tales about Buffalo Bill Cody, Kit Carson, and Calamity Jane, dime novelists turned these individuals into national celebrities. Factual exploits were mixed with legends and boasts and then also with Eastern fantasies about the West to create the equivalent of comic-book superheroes who happened to be labeled with the names of actual people.

Liver-eating Johnston did not receive such an honor. Perhaps his legend was too gruesome or his personality too prickly. Indeed, non–mountain men tended to see him as a pariah. One source noted that at the Musselshell, he stood "a half-naked beast hurling obscenities at Missouri steamboat passengers as they gawked at the cannibal on shore beside his thirty-odd bleached Indian skulls."

Johnston was even willing to stand by and be proclaimed a monster to children—"Be a good boy, or he'll come cut out your liver and eat it!" This is something the vain and self-promoting Cody never would have abided. Indeed, only Johnston could have gotten away with greeting Cody by saying, "Buffalo Bill, the Indian fighter, the only Indian you ever put your hands on was a squaw!"

But if Johnston wasn't admired or even recognized by the country as a whole, that only made him more of a hero among his subculture. Mountain men continued puffing up his legend, and by the 1890s it was being cited by novelists, journalists, and folklorists who claimed to be countering the dime novelists in capturing a *real* West. For both the mountain men and their chroniclers, the fact that these stories were "undiscovered" made them more "authentic"—perhaps even true.

They were, almost certainly, not true. Late in his life, Johnston wrote that he had never married an Indian woman. No evidence exists of any vendetta against Crows, only friendship. (In honor of his size and hairiness, the Crows called him Black Bear.) And though Johnston did claim he had killed and scalped the Sioux warrior, he noted that a piece of flesh stuck to his knife accidentally and that he wiped it off before pretending to eat it in a show for his friends.

As he passed the age of seventy, Johnston settled down a bit. By 1897, he had received a patent on a homestead south of Red Lodge, where he tended a garden and hayfield. He served as that mining town's first constable. He was still a fearsome man, capable of breaking up a fight by knocking the brawlers' heads together. But he was also affectionately known as "Dad" Johnston.

His tenure in Red Lodge was short. In December 1899, after he was bedridden for three weeks, friends secured him a place in an old-soldiers' home in California. Six weeks later he passed away.

THROUGH THE TWENTIETH century, the legends of Liver-eating Johnston gradually came into print. Eventually they also made it onto film. The 1972 movie *Jeremiah Johnson* starred the young Robert Redford as a misanthropic trapper drawn into a painful one-man war with the Crow tribe. It was largely believed to be based on Liver-eater's life rather than the legends that had grown up around that life.

The movie brought attention to the mountain-man era, prompting a study by Tri Robinson's seventh-grade class in Lancaster, California. That's when they discovered the underwhelming location of Johnston's grave and decided to do something about it. They found indications that Johnston had asked to be buried near his home in Red Lodge. So they wrote to state governments and historical societies in Montana and Wyoming, as well as the Veterans' Administration.

The best response they got was from Old Trail Town, a tourist attraction that reconstructed a pioneer village west of Cody, Wyoming. Old Trail Town volunteered to help with costs of the reburial and give Johnston a grand Fourth of July (re-)sendoff. Representatives from Montana were, for some reason, slower to respond.

Perhaps they believed the federal government would never go along. One Red Lodge historian wrote that the disinterment violated several Veterans' Administration regulations. Even Cody leaders later said they weren't sure anything was going to happen until they got word one day in mid-1974: the body was on its way.

At that point Red Lodge went to work, putting in its own claim to house the remains of its former lawman. Red Lodge leaders asked their congressman,

John Melcher, to confront the Wyoming congressional delegation and the VA. Soon they asked for a federal court injunction to stop the Cody ceremony. The body, Robinson says, had to be hidden for weeks while the debates were sorted out.

The feud became a media spectacle. When Cody finally won the legal battle, Redford journeyed to Wyoming to serve as a pallbearer. Mindful of the way a Colorado community had snookered them out of Buffalo Bill's grave back in 1918, Codyites made sure this body would stay put by packing the crypt with two truckloads of concrete. Meanwhile, several of the eulogists referred to the deceased as Jeremiah Johnson.

AND PERHAPS THAT'S for the best: to have buried the outsized legends under a false name at a tourist attraction in a town the man had barely known. For that can free the real Johnston from the legends that overwhelmed him.

In his old age, he was honored and treasured in part because few Euro-Americans had lived in Montana for so long, in part because that tenure had required such strength and character, and in part because he was willing to tell magnificent stories.

One winter, he claimed, he had killed and eaten thirteen bison, so prodigious was his appetite. During the flight of the Nez Perce in 1877, he claimed, he'd been a scout for the Seventh Cavalry, but higher-ups had ignored his advice not to be fooled by the Indians' feint toward the Stinkingwater. On a steamboat in 1869, he said, he'd been puzzled and a little afraid of an oddly cold substance called "ice cream"; asking his buddy where it came from, he received the answer, "It come in cans!" While serving as a deputy sheriff in Coulson (the settlement that preceded Billings), he said, he'd been asked why he made so few arrests and responded that since "there ain't no jail here to put 'em in after I arrest 'em…I just beat the hell out of the ones that should be arrested and turn 'em loose, and I've never had to arrest the same man twice!"

Such stories, even more than the inflated notions of slaughtering Indians or eating livers, capture the hardships and joys of nineteenth-century Montana living and the character of some of the folks who lived through that time. What's more, it seems unlikely that such a character would put much stock in the location of a pine box containing bodily remains. He'd be more likely to believe in a notion that seems appropriate to many of us today as well: a lasting spirit roaming freely through the mountains.

Montana Quarterly, 2006

Resurrecting Haydie Yates

In 1927, in a regular *New Yorker* magazine feature titled "Why I Like New York," a writer named Haydie Cox commended a taxi driver who pulled up next to a dray horse that was struggling to eat oats with its bridle still in its mouth. "The chauffeur leaped out of the car, snatched the bridle from the horse's head, [and] hung it on the harness hame," she wrote, referring to the part of the harness that goes around the horse's neck. "'Excuse the delay,'" the driver said, and explained that a previous employer insisted that he look after such animals' comfort.

In many ways the piece was unremarkable, a standard breezy vignette of life in New York, written in the magazine's typical literary style. But in other ways it *was* remarkable: not only for its subject (a *horse* in 1927 Manhattan?) but also for its author. Haydie Cox was the first female reporter for this famous "Talk of the Town" section. And she would soon trade writing about horses for riding them. Before the end of the year, she would marry Frederick "Ted" Yates, vacation in Europe, drive a Model T Ford across the country to southern Montana, and purchase a small ranch on Lodge Grass Creek.

We should know a great deal about Haydie and her outlook on life because she wrote about her ranch experiences in the wonderful memoir *70 Miles from a Lemon*. (The title referred to the long journey from the ranch to their grocer in Sheridan, Wyoming.) Sadly, however, with the book long out of print, Haydie has faded from Montana's literary consciousness. It's time to bring her back to life.

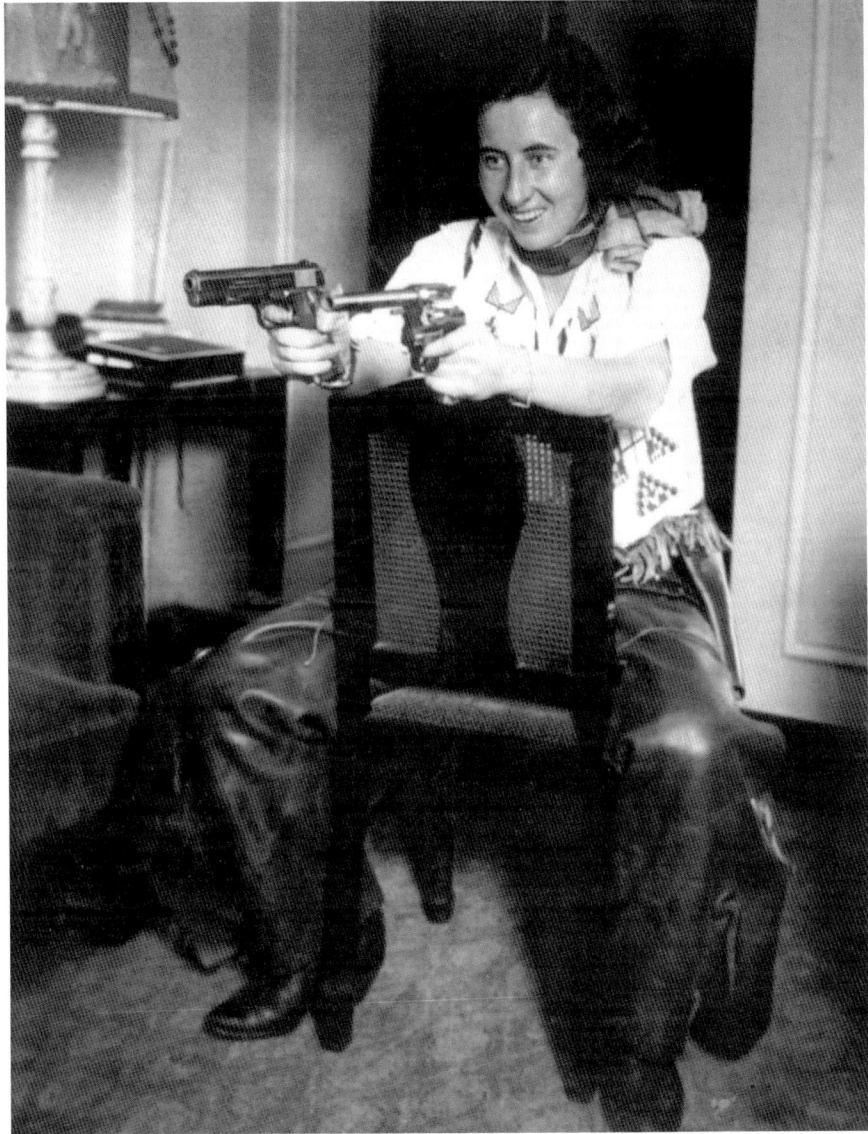

Haydie Yates, shown here in full "dudine" regalia, owned a ranch on Lodge Grass Creek from 1927 to 1934 and later wrote a captivating memoir about that time. *Courtesy Angus Yates.*

EMMA HAYDEN EAMES was born in Connecticut in 1897 to an accomplished, well-to-do family. Her aunt, also named Emma Eames (hence the youngster's nickname "Haydie"), was a world-famous opera singer. Haydie's older sister Clare would grow up to be an actress, married to future Academy Award–

winning screenwriter Sidney Howard. Haydie spent her childhood years in Maryland and Ohio. But in 1917, she decided to spend a summer at the Valley Ranch outside of Cody, Wyoming.

Irving H. "Larry" Larom, owner of the Valley Ranch, was a leader in the new enterprise of dude ranching. Larom used his Princeton University connections to bring wealthy, well-bred young people to the South Fork of the Shoshone River for a summer of riding, fishing, hunting, and touring. The dudes and dudines (as they were then called) were not able to travel in Europe because of the war and wanted something more active than stuffy Eastern resorts.

Haydie in particular really took to it. She acquired the nickname "Cactus Kate" and made friends widely among both vacationers and Cody's permanent residents. She returned four summers in a row and concluded the fourth one with a wedding to fellow Easterner Arthur "Bud" Cox at her family home in Cleveland. When the *Cody Enterprise* wrote about the impending nuptials, it provided a sense of Haydie's personality: "We haven't heard, but rather expect the ceremony to be performed by a sky-pilot in a plug hat, two six-guns, and a red bandana. The bride's costume, doubtless will consist of a beaded vest, red shirt, and blue overalls. As for the groom—well, grooms don't matter much in weddings." The following month Haydie served as a bridesmaid at Larom's wedding to the city librarian, and then the Coxes set up their own nearby dude ranch, the N E.

The marriage did not last. But that didn't slow Haydie down. In 1926, she bought her own ranch on the South Fork, announcing that she intended to spend summers there. Perhaps emboldened by the sense of equality she experienced in the West, by the winter of 1927 she was back in New York, working at the famous magazine.

Ted Yates, who had attended Yale and fought in World War I, had also been a Cody-area dude. But when the new couple returned to Wyoming, they decided to explore a new area, first examining Sheridan. On the drive out, she later wrote, "the heavy, crowded, self-conscious world of the East went into reverse. Cities, full of Rotary, misguided good works, and worry…And suddenly on the sixth day were the Rockies standing up before us in purple and gold." They found a 3,200-acre parcel on the east slope of the Bighorn Mountains, just north of the Montana border on the Crow Reservation, and bought it for $2,400.

In her memoir, Haydie was particularly good at writing about that classic theme of the West, independence. For example, she discussed a conversation she had with an old surveyor, who told her that what everybody wanted was "freedom." Asked how he defined that word, he told her, "Why, it's hoein' your own row in your own sweet way, for better, for worse. It's even the right to go to hell in your own handbasket."

Yet Haydie would soon learn exactly what that "for worse" meant in this country. During the first long, cold winter in a little house they'd constructed on the grasslands, she wrote, "Most of our treasure of canned goods had exploded like a Fourth of July celebration with the first real freeze."

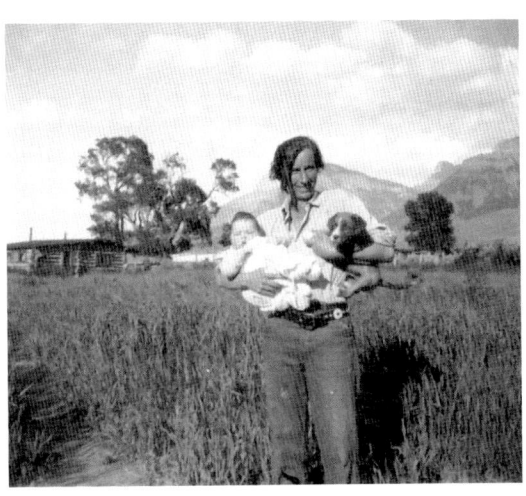

Haydie Yates holds her infant son Ted and a puppy on her ranch at the foot of the Bighorns. She did not seek to "civilize" the West but to revel in it. *Courtesy Angus Yates.*

Which meant, some weeks later, that dinners were not always appetizing: "On the stove the large open kettle stewed a pallid soup, into which [a hired man] at intervals would shy frozen potatoes and turnips to keep company with the piece of venison which, being the soul and body of the stew, no one ate and had now acquired a vivid resemblance to an old sneaker."

Yet she found it worthwhile. Of a winter evening, she wrote: "Then we would sit, me on the bunk and Ted in the big chair, and wonder whether it was cozier to be inside, dry and warm, looking out at a Montana winter, or outside, cold and wind-blown, looking in at warmth and comfort which was ours to enjoy."

WHEN HISTORIANS WRITE about the dude-ranching era, they often emphasize two points: first, that the dudines were escaping very strict gender roles in the East, and second, that many of them so enjoyed the West that they stayed. What's particularly interesting about Haydie Yates is how she combines the best of these phenomena.

There can be little doubt that Haydie, who had a kewpie doll tattooed on her thigh, did not fit the strictures of post-Victorian formality. The newspaper's image of Haydie's preferred wedding attire suggests how much she took to cowboy chic. Yet Haydie also took to the responsibilities that came with this freedom. This was not merely a Halloween costume. Living in the West meant hard work—and gender or class background did not excuse you from it.

On the ranch, Haydie wanted to be accepted by the men who worked alongside her; she knew that meant she had to meet them on their terms. In *70 Miles*, she wrote, "Anonymity of gender can be maintained only by insisting on a share and share alike of all hard work and hardship and being rather on the modest side in asking relief or comfort. If you fail to follow this basic precept, unless you are very beautiful, you're a bloody bore."

So when she decided to settle in Montana and raise Hereford cattle, she brought with her few of the worries or self-consciousness of her previous life. She was not seeking to "civilize" the West, but to revel in it. For example, she was not much for trails: "Only the simon-pure tenderfoot gets himself lost... He has a weakness for following the familiar landmarks of civilized travel. To him a long-unused logging road is irresistible, even though it leads in the wrong direction...The sight of a trail is like the sight of dope to an addict. Hotly he pursues it to its end at a salt lick or a game wallow. Experience and common sense will one day tell him that creeks are his signposts and the bare ridges which parallel them are his roads."

Pregnant during the winter of 1930–31, Haydie moved to town, staying at the Sheridan Inn, which she described as "the gathering place of ranchers, state politicians, pensioners of one sort or another, rich ne'er-do-wells, spinster schoolmarms, dudes in expensive buckskins and dudines in fringe and fashionable permanents, sourdoughs, old-timers, and jolly rumrunners...The narrow dark halls were perpetually whirling with drifting eddies of people going in and out of each other's rooms."

From her position of means, she celebrated that mixture of people as a sort of classless society, an American ideal reinforced by the beautiful but difficult landscape. The following winter she had a job at the Sheridan newspaper and described the town as "the Nob Hill among the Rockies' peaks. They were the sons, nephews, nieces, and uncles of dukes and earls or earls in their own right...Not that they cared. There was no ounce of snob about them...The members of this recherché group were interesting individuals and real."

The frontier was fading. The worst thing about living on Lodge Grass Creek at the foot of the Bighorns was not the danger of outlaws or Indian attack or a bear mauling or starvation, not the cold or the wind or the isolation or a lack of career opportunities—it was the fact that if you had a hankering for citrus, you had to travel seventy miles to get it.

And as that frontier faded, Haydie and her cohorts lived out a sort of American Dream for the society that might replace it.

Although Haydie wrote about several of her neighbors, she didn't say much about Native Americans. A product of her segregated times, she probably didn't really "see" Indians as individuals. The West eroded barriers of gender and class but was less successful with race—even though her ranch was on the reservation.

She did see enough of her Crow neighbors to describe their overall difficulties with incredible insight and courage for the time. "Sixty years in a glorified concentration camp, spoon-fed and tyrannized over by an ill-qualified though no doubt benevolent Congress and a bureaucracy whose very existence depends on the Indians' continued segregation from the march of time, was hardly warranted to give them twentieth-century sea legs."

In 1934, federal Indian policy changed. So did federal grazing policy. Though these policies shouldn't directly affect private landholders such as Haydie and Ted (now joined by the infant Teddy and her son from her previous marriage, Eames), they did create uncertainty. How would they affect the Yateses' grazing and water rights, now also potentially influenced by a Native American superintendent, the first to be put in charge of his own tribal agency? On top of Depression and drought, it was enough to convince Haydie and family to return to New York.

Other factors may also have played a role. When Haydie asked three-year-old Teddy what he wanted for Christmas, she claimed he responded, "I want a buckskin son-of-a-bitch with a black mane and a long wavery tail." As much as she enjoyed the affable earthiness of the ranch hands, she may have also wanted more sophisticated influences on her child. (At this she succeeded: he became a legendary television news producer.)

Haydie continued to live vibrantly. She rose to top editorial positions at three New York women's magazines in rapid succession. A *Newsweek* article described her as having "done about everything that vigorous femininity tackles." And that was before *70 Miles from a Lemon*, which came out in 1948. Sadly, a few years later Haydie took ill in Florida and died at age fifty-three.

It was a loss to the world, but especially to Montana and Wyoming. She might not have come back: as she said toward the end of the book, "No other place out there could ever be as much our hearts' desire as that perfect spot on the Lodgegrass." But she could have carried forth her memories of that golden time, when mixed together on that perfect spot were men and women, dudes and cowhands, earls and sourdoughs, with the drifting eddies of them all coming together as equals under the Bighorns.

Magic City, 2013

AT THE LITTLE BIGHORN

"I always hear people speak in whispers here, like they're in a church," Gerard Baker, superintendent of the Little Bighorn Battlefield National Monument, told me in 1993. "In many national parks you'll talk about different things, loud and excited, but this place invokes an almost religious attitude."

The attitude makes sense at a memorial battlefield, a cemetery, the spot where General George Armstrong Custer made his famous Last Stand in a battle with Sioux, Cheyenne, and other Indian warriors. And on my visit I wanted to understand and appreciate that attitude. But I also wanted to understand and appreciate Baker, a Native American taking over as head of this place of such significance to our memory of the nineteenth-century racial clashes.

The 1874 discovery of gold in South Dakota's Black Hills brought thousands of whites to sacred Native ground, violating an 1868 treaty. In frustration and defiance, the Sioux and Cheyenne raided settlements and travelers in the area. Custer's troops were part of an effort to punish and contain the Indians.

On the Little Bighorn River on June 25, 1876, Custer stumbled across one of the largest gatherings of Plains Indians ever—more than seven thousand people, including two thousand warriors. Underestimating their size and power, he divided his regiment into three battalions and attacked. The Indians, including Sitting Bull, Crazy Horse, and other now-famous warriors, easily beat back two of the battalions (under Major Marcus Reno

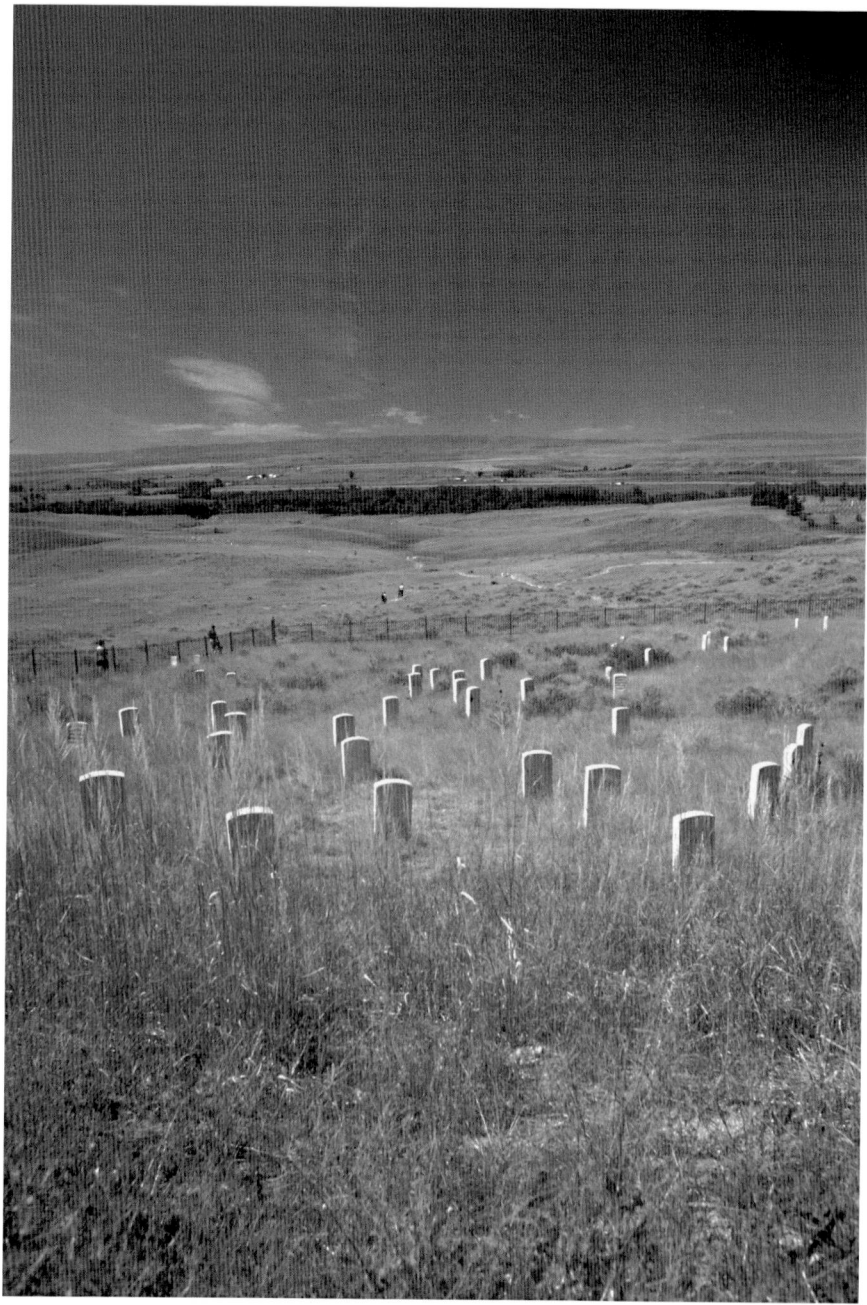

At the Little Bighorn National Battlefield, simple stones enhance the mystical properties of the landscape, building a haunting spirituality. *National Park Service photo.*

and Captain Frederick Benteen). They then surrounded and destroyed Custer's troops and laid siege to the Reno-Benteen faction for two more days before withdrawing.

"What happened here in the two days of the battle was very violent," Baker said. "It was a very violent ending to some people's lives, both Indian and white." Visitors to this day get that sense; the mystical properties of the land are enhanced by simple stones marking where the bodies of soldiers were found.

But the character of the Little Bighorn, and its reflection in the silence of visitors, goes deeper than that of a simple cemetery. "It represents a time period in American history that was an end conflict between two cultures," Baker said. "So it offers visitors—both Indian and non-Indian—a chance to open a door for them to explore their own culture plus another culture. What really happened? It wasn't just the fact that people met here for two days in June of 1876. And that they had a battle and one group lost. There were all sorts of events leading up to it."

Baker, who is Mandan-Hidatsa, has had a lifelong fascination with Native history and culture. So he has thought a lot about how the Little Bighorn figured in the region's history. He notes that it was one of the Indians' biggest individual triumphs over the U.S. military and also what that military represented: the whole European expansion to the West.

"If you're on the Indian side, you could say, 'We won that one, that was really good.' But look what happened afterward: we're still on the reservations, we still have poverty, unemployment, suicides, a high rate of death. And on the other side, the white side, people say, 'Those Indians are bad for massacring all of our soldiers, for having the bodies stripped and cut up.' What this place offers them is a chance to understand why that happened, what evolved in our history to make these people so mad."

They were losing their homeland, their lifestyle, their culture. And this is the other remarkable quality about the Little Bighorn Battlefield, a reason people stay so quiet: the place still calls up the spirit and character of the land that held and nurtured that culture.

From Custer Hill, the spot of the Last Stand, you look southwest across the valley of the Little Bighorn, or "Greasy Grass," as the Indians called the river. And if you can take a mental eraser to the asphalt strips of Interstate 90, the area seems to have changed not at all. You can easily conjure an image of the thousand lodges that made up the Indian village on the west side of the river in late June 1876. Looking far to the west, to the Pryor Mountains, or looking east across the open rangeland, you can easily conjure images of prairie ruled by buffalo—the power and freedom of life on the plains.

"There was a big difference in those days in the relationship to the land between Indians and whites," Baker said. "Indians believed then, and still somewhat to this day, that there is a Spirit and everything is alive. That made it easier to defend your land to the death, because you were, basically, defending your mother."

Baker is a genial man. But when asked, he said that had he been born 150 years ago, he would have been one of the warriors. "I would have defended my country. I would have defended my land, my family, my children. We had this freedom to roam, go where we wanted to go. It was a loss of an area for the people. If you concentrate just on the battle, rather than the forces leading up to it, you lose that understanding."

And so, even in the personal admission, he circles back to education: the value of the Little Bighorn as a gateway to cultural understanding. "People can learn the Indian culture, what they went through. And at the same time, they can learn why the military was coming in, what was their purpose. Their purpose was to say to the Indians that people are coming, western expansion—there's nothing you can do about it. They're farming, they're ranching. The old days are over."

Though the old days may be over, their effects continue to be felt. "We still have battles today," Baker said about the Little Bighorn. The very name of the monument was a source of controversy when it was changed from "Custer Battlefield" in late 1991. In 1993, concerns arose over a private enterprise's plans to build a "living history" park just outside the monument's borders, under a contractual agreement with the National Park Service. Did it amount to the selling of a national treasure?

Baker finds those battles, or at least the passion behind them, healthy. He attributes it to the same cause as the silence of the visitors: the haunting spirituality still invoked by those powerful events of over one hundred years ago. Emotions run high because people feel so strongly about this piece of land. "That atmosphere," he said. "I don't think it'll ever leave this place."

To me, Baker is a wonderful character of Montana history. It seems funny to call a child of the 1950s a character of history, but Baker is both a character and a man who can explain and represent Montana history. Throughout his personal and professional lives he has sought to bridge the cultural gap between white and native cultures. In his job at the battlefield,

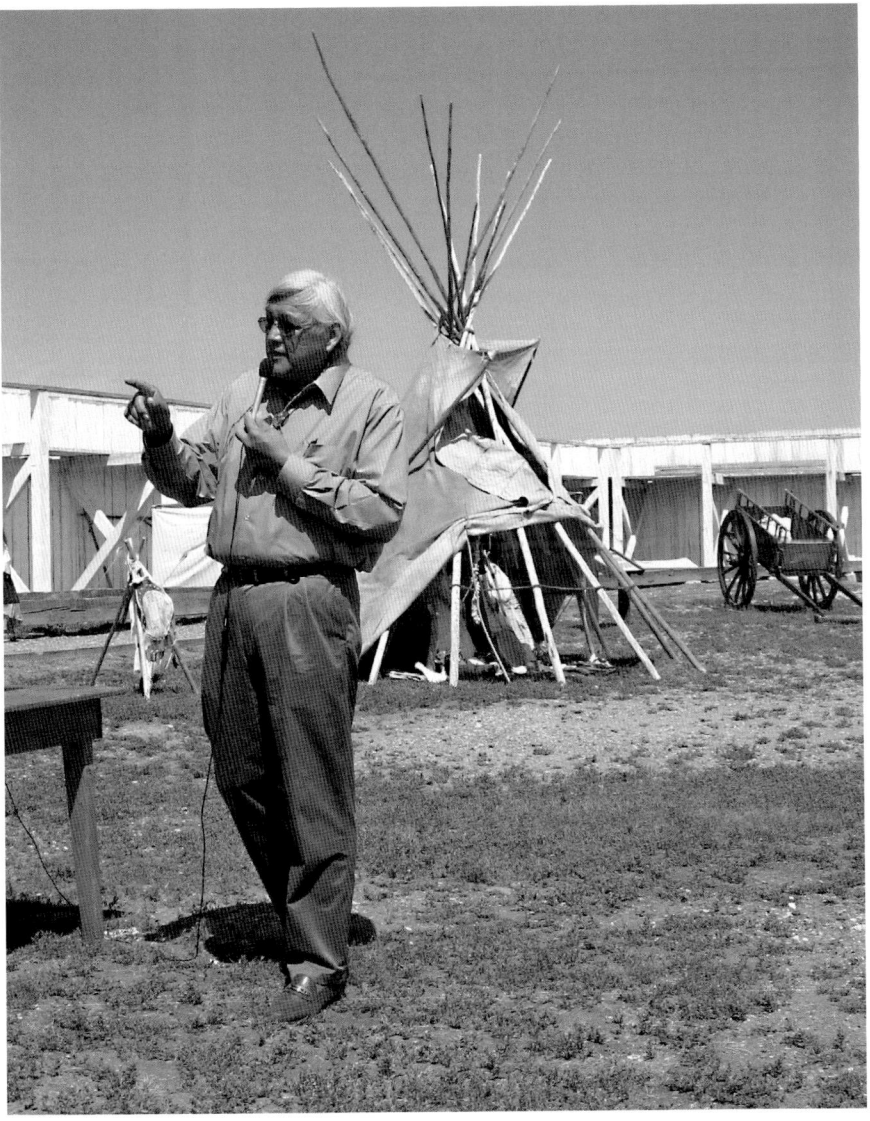

Gerard Baker, shown here lecturing at Fort Union National Historic Site, was the superintendent at the Little Bighorn Battlefield in the early 1990s. His lengthy, prestigious Park Service career sought to ease prejudice through education. *National Park Service photo.*

he superintended a monument to the perils of that gap, the toll it can take on both sides.

Baker's ascent to the job is an inspiring story, for a person who was raised on a reservation in North Dakota, in a log house with no running water and no electricity, by parents who had not completed high school but vowed that their four children would all graduate from college. It even sounds like a true-life Horatio Alger story.

Baker, however, was uncomfortable with the notion that his experience epitomized one of white America's most cherished myths: work hard and succeed. Because culturally and philosophically, he considers himself very much a Mandan-Hidatsa. For example, he started telling about his childhood—long before mentioning the rustic elements of the cabin—by saying, "I was brought up by a lot of the old people. We had an extended family. I got to learn a lot of the oral history. And that's what established my philosophy, that I still go by, listening to my parents and my clan grandfathers.

"We can no longer live the old way, they'd say. We can no longer hunt buffalo, we can no longer live in earth lodges or tipis, we can longer exist as we did a long time ago. And what they said to me was that you have to understand the white man's way. But at the same time never forget who you are. Always keep your culture."

The key, Baker learned, was to adapt. "We may no longer live in a warrior society, we may not be able to go on the warpath, but we can live the old way in philosophy. We can have enemies. My enemy now is my paperwork, and my way to overcome this enemy is to do it, logically, as best as I possibly can. This is just a different way of functioning as a warrior."

Baker's reverence for the old people, the old ways, started early. "Our clan—like most Indian cultures—felt it was very important to have family around, all the time. There was always somebody at our house, visiting. And when I was very young, seventh grade, I started an oral history program. Just for myself, basically. Taping some of the old people. All of them are gone now, including my father. But I still have the tapes. And my mother, who is eighty-one, is still teaching me."

And his passion for history served him well in his early career. He got a degree in criminology, because the easiest way into the Park Service at that time was through law enforcement. But, stationed at the Theodore Roosevelt National Park in North Dakota, he got involved in interpretation. "There was a need, on the Anglo side," he said, "to learn about Indian culture. I saw a lot of racism around, and I have always believed the root of racism is not knowing one another." He worked as a historian at the Knife River Indian Villages and Fort Union Trading Post before taking over as administrator for the north unit of the Roosevelt park.

Baker has a gentle nature that seems at odds with his husky six-foot-five-inch frame. He's gregarious, quick with a smile, and a natural storyteller.

"I love to visit with people," he commented. Those traits, along with his passion and knowledge, have served him well as a media representative. He's been featured in documentaries and books on Native and regional culture. (After our interview, he went on to several high-profile positions in the Park Service, retiring in 2012.)

In one of those books, the bestselling *Great Plains*, Ian Frazier wrote, "If anyone nowadays could be called a genuine plainsman, it is Gerard Baker." The proclamation made Baker uncomfortable. "Culturally, our people are not braggarts, individualists," he said. "We're part of a unit, a clanship. Now, he [Frazier] met me at a time in my life when I was really into the living history of it…"

Indeed, Frazier wrote rhapsodically of Baker showing him dozens of cultural artifacts, providing him with all sorts of historical information, taking him out to throw a double-bladed axe, and inviting him to join in a sweat bath. Though what's truly remarkable is that Baker would have done this with anybody, not just a big Eastern writer. Indeed, one friend claims that despite his significant role in the book, Baker has only the vaguest memories of Frazier's visit—the experiences simply weren't that unusual for him.

Removing the superlative, however, Baker accepted the appellation "plainsman." "I enjoy open areas, sunsets, sunrises," he said. "And the plains invoke a sense of freedom for me." Before moving to the battlefield, he spent three years with the Custer National Forest in mountainous Red Lodge. "I missed the sunsets, seeing a long ways away. Being out here brings me closer to home, to my tribe."

Baker has always done a lot of public speaking, to professional groups wanting to learn more about Native American culture, and to schools, both Indian and non-Indian. "I think it's real important to fill in some of the gaps we have," he said, "to ease prejudice through education." With Native American kids, he talks again of that philosophy of his elders: how to adapt their culture to the white man's ways. "Our enemy is not the white man," he'll say. "My enemy, over the years, in many different ways, has been myself. You can look at the school system as an enemy if you want, as long as you do it in a positive sense: something you have to learn and conquer."

And with any audience, his message is that he's nobody special. "You know, people will say to me, 'You've done so much with your life,' implying, 'You are Indian but you're different from other Indian people.' And I'm not different than any other Indian people. That accusation really bothers me, because it involves so many misconceptions: that Indian people live on welfare, that we all get checks every month, free medical care and education.

We don't. And I'm no different from anybody on my reservation. Here's what I always tell the kids: they need to set goals for themselves and then achieve them."

It sounds like such a simple philosophy. And yet, coming from a man who has gained so many complex achievements, it also rings utterly true.

Montana Magazine, 1994

The Native Home of Governors on Horseback

If you heard about the man who kicked off his campaign to become governor of Montana by swinging a medieval battle sword on horseback in the middle of downtown Billings, you probably thought, "Only in the American West."

Such a thing could happen only in a region so caught up with cowboys and horses, so eager to see them as more than vocation or transportation, so willing to hand over important policy decisions to a man who speaks in such symbols. Only in the West could a potential candidate have sat down to think about how to go after the most important job in his state and apparently concluded, "Well, first I need a horse. Then maybe a weapon." Only in the West could such a candidate expect to be taken seriously.

And Glenn Schaffer was taken a tiny bit seriously. In February 2004, he posed at the offices of the *Billings Gazette* on a white stallion named Big Dog Thunder Horse and said that his campaign motto would be "Honor, Above All Else." He cited Hannibal, the Carthaginian general, as his example. Announcing that he would campaign across Montana with his horse, he said, "I will not ask for money, but for water and shelter for me and my steed."

The *Gazette* put his story on the front page.

I couldn't fault the newspaper. I found it a tremendously readable story. Partly, I found it refreshing to have a candidate for statewide office admit his ignorance about the economy and promise only to try to set a good example. Furthermore, his platforms of reducing the cost of child care and building public respect for law enforcement officers made a lot more sense to me than anything the outgoing governor had done. And I was delighted to read a political story that wasn't analyzing the candidate's fundraising strengths or intraparty reputation.

But then it wasn't really a political story. It was clearly pitched as human interest, a fascinating local individual involved in an unusual enterprise. Glenn Schaffer, the *Gazette* was saying, was a typical Montana character. You can understand a lot about a region by looking at the human-interest stories that run on the front pages of a local newspaper.

In this case, the story made me happy to be a Westerner. I was glad to live in a region that had such a clear sense of itself. Schaffer didn't strike me as any less ridiculous a gubernatorial candidate than Jesse Ventura—but where the former Minnesota governor had made his reputation as a professional wrestler, we had a cowboy. While both professions involve a good deal of symbolic good and evil and both make for fun Halloween costumes, in that outfit, the genuine cowboy can earn a real if paltry paycheck.

I didn't vote for Glenn Schaffer. He never filed the paperwork to be listed as an official candidate, never even followed through on his plans to announce a running mate chosen "not on the basis of a resume, but on spirit, heart and soul. It would help to have someone with experience in the legislature." He had his fifteen minutes of fame on the front page of the *Gazette* and then disappeared.

But I've kept thinking about his story, based largely on a tiny little hard-to-reconcile fact buried deep in the original article: when he mounted that horse in downtown Billings, Schaffer had lived in Montana only four years.

I'VE COME TO see Glenn Schaffer as important not because of anything he did in politics but because he represents an underappreciated trend: it's the newcomers who feed off of (and thus feed) our Western myths.

Do you see the West as the frontier, a place where you can reinvent yourself? Then you're probably from the East. Do you equate wilderness with unspoiled purity? Then chances are you're from a coastal city. Do you see the concept of honor on horseback as proving your electability? Then maybe you're a recent migrant from Pennsylvania.

Certainly when I moved West at age twenty-six, I was gung-ho for the mountain image. I immediately bought cross-country skis and a mountain bike. I acquired a dog and hiked with her constantly. I felt inferior for not being a rock-climber, telemark skier, or winter backpacker. I was reinventing my life, emphasizing and even discovering the activities and character traits that represented the "real" me, which had been unfairly suppressed by my previous residence. Every time I found more of the real me in the West, my spirit surged with delight.

But then I met Montanans who hadn't made the two-hour drive to Yellowstone in decades.

As a newcomer in a small town, I quickly volunteered to serve on boards and committees to preserve and strengthen our community. And I soon learned that without the newcomers' enthusiasm, many such organizations would wither and die.

I developed a passion for Western literature. Then I met my wife, who grew up in eastern Montana, and learned that she prefers Dostoevsky.

Friends tell me of similar situations around the West: In Wyoming, newcomers embrace the horse-packing image; in New Mexico, they build in adobe; in southern Utah, they follow the Ed Abbey legends. It's the people from elsewhere who most love and sustain the old myths.

The more time I spend here, the more I alter my picture of typical Westerners, the ones whose character is no longer defined by where they *used* to live. (When exactly you cross that line—after thirty years of residence? only if you're native-born?—is a question for another essay.) The more time they've been out West, the less they're defined by horses or cowboys or wilderness or quaint small-town cafés. Many of the ones I've met prefer snowmobiles, four-wheelers, Harleys, or similarly motorized updates to those clunky romantic traditions. Many need economic development and see wilderness as an obstacle to it that puts their region at a disadvantage compared to the rest of the nation. Many want the sort of good-tasting food that's ubiquitous in California and believe they can find it at an Olive Garden.

In other words, many Westerners want…what everyone else in the country wants. The longer you've lived out here, the more you've done without the latest trends and conveniences, the more aggravated you may become at their absence. Ask a harried corporate executive what she most wants out of life, and she may say she wants to be a cowgirl. Ask a woman herding cattle, and she may say she wants cellphone coverage so she can be better connected to the world while on roundup.

I'm not saying this is good or bad, just inevitable. Progress—the antimythology—is as much desired in the West as anywhere else. Distinguishing the West from other regions, to my mind, are two factors. One is that our wide-open spaces cause that progress to arrive here more slowly than elsewhere. But although some people mistake slow-to-arrive change for a lack of change, this difference doesn't impact our culture as much as the second difference: the West is full of newcomers who are attracted by the old-time mythologies.

You might move to Atlanta for a job. You might move to New York for the museums. You might move to rural Missouri because of a family connection. In any of those cases, you'll still embrace progress. But the West has a far greater percentage than any other region of people who arrive because of a mythology of the past. They love horses and come to a place where the horse dominates. They love wilderness and come to a place where they can experience it regularly. They love John Wayne, or Hunter S. Thompson, or Georgia O'Keefe, and want to live in a region that hasn't progressed past identifying with their idol.

Yes, I'm speaking in broad generalizations here, but I do so for a reason: it's really interesting when the stereotypes meet. These myth-obsessed newcomers don't have the power to stop progress in its tracks—nobody does—but their efforts to do so create an exciting tension. Just as wildlife finds the intersection of two ecosystems (say, forest and meadow) to be the richest habitat, I find this intersection of myth and anti-myth to be a vibrant culture, a place I want to live.

Let me explain it with an example. When he taught in the environmental studies program at the University of Montana, Don Snow told me he thought the school's great reputation came from the way it took kids who thought they were environmentalists and turned them into Montanans. I took him to mean that the environmentalists had come with a starry-eyed view of nature and its essential goodness and suddenly been surrounded by practical, friendly Montanans with a bias toward getting things done. In other words, both archetypes have value, but the most substantial value comes when either is exposed to the opposite perspective.

That's what I'd like to think the West as a region tends to do as well. It takes people who thought they were cowboys, or skiers, or loggers, or hippies, or miners, or outdoor-recreation junkies, or budding real-estate moguls, or…whatever they came to the West for—and turns them into Westerners, which is something less romantic but more functional. We are, all of us in the region, caught somewhere in that transformation. We live at the intersection of myth and reality, and everybody gets entertainingly confused as to which street is which.

When Glenn Schaffer gets on his horse to run for office, he's part of that mix. When the *Billings Gazette* (and, for that matter, I myself) report with such glee on people like him, so are we. We are yet another set of relative newcomers reinvigorating Western mythology. In Schaffer's case, many of us are saying, "Isn't the West full of unusual characters?"

It doesn't matter whether the West really has any more unusual characters per capita than anywhere else. The point is that people like me want it to. My belief that the West is full of unusual characters—like others' beliefs that it's full of cowboys, or wilderness, or individualism—fuels the very culture we seek. Merely by pursuing our mythic dreams, we perpetuate them.

Tying my personal view that "characters" are the ultimate Western mythology to an individual named Glenn Schaffer may make you think I celebrate this guy only because I think he's a bit of a wacko. That's not entirely the case. What I admired about the *Gazette*'s article was the way it showed Schaffer grasping the heroic elements of the Western vision. I saw direct parallels to 102 years previously, when another Pennsylvanian also grafted the concept of honor onto a horseman and paraded that image around in the media. In that previous case, Owen Wister dubbed his creation *The Virginian*, and publication of his novel did much to enshrine what we now think of as the cowboy myth.

Wister did it because he fell in love with a region of epic landscapes, big and bold enough to support mythic constructions that he consciously modeled on stories of the Bible and King Arthur. Wister couldn't imagine *The Virginian* happening in the Pennsylvania of 1902 any more than I could have imagined the grand spiritual structure of the life I wanted to live happening in the Massachusetts of 1990.

We may occasionally bump into the limits of those visions. We may forget that the West is not entirely peopled by taciturn, honorable men riding the open range, nor by idealistic granola-crunchers leaving no trace. That forgetfulness may lead us to enact policies that reduce our quality of life. But even then, we do still have those epic landscapes. If in another 102 years they are not still inspiring newcomers to run for governor on horseback, I believe they will still be inspiring similarly heroic characters to similarly deep spiritual quests, in pursuit of the reflections they see on those landscapes of qualities of the human soul—qualities of goodwill, honor, and hope.

High Country News, 2004
West of 98: Living and Writing the New American West, 2011

Acknowledgements

Like many nonfiction writers, I have huge personal debts to a wide variety of people who provided stories, perspectives, and opportunities. I hope these pages effectively represent the views of my interviewees and sources. Furthermore, like many books, this one is a product of not just research but also life, and thus reflects the contributions of the many people who have touched my life over the last (mumble-mumble) years. I'll call out just a few of the most obvious here.

Thanks to Will McKay, who first approached me with the idea of this collection. And thanks to his colleagues at The History Press, who have made the publishing process rapid and smooth.

Thanks to the editors who initially worked with me on these essays, including Beverly Magley, Butch Larcombe, and Sheila Habeck at *Montana Magazine*; Megan Ault Regnerus and Scott McMillion at the *Montana Quarterly*; Paul Larmer and Betsy Marston at *High Country News* and its Writers on the Range series (thanks also to all the newspaper editors who picked up my pieces from that syndicate); Clark Whitehorn and Molly Holz at *Montana: The Magazine of Western History*; Allyn Hulteng at *Magic City*; Michele Dill at *Horizon Air*; Don Snow at the *Chronicle of Community*; and Russell Rowland on the book *West of 98*. Some writers like to complain about editors, but I found these people to be thoughtful, generous, and a genuine help to my career.

Thanks to Dave Stauffer, Susan Bury, and Gary Ferguson, whose manuscript reviews led to several improvements (all remaining errors, of course, remain my own responsibility). Thanks to Angus Yates, Senia Hart,

Acknowledgements

Liza McClelland, Tressa Fahrenthold, and David Kallenbach for providing copyrighted photographs; thanks also to the Library of Congress, National Park Service, states of Montana and Wyoming, and Wikimedia for making available high-resolution public domain images.

Thanks to the people who shared their stories with me, including those quoted in the book and those (such as the late Hal Rothman) who "merely" shaped my thinking that went into these pieces. Thanks to the Matthew Hansen endowment, which paid some of my expenses researching "Hope and Bacon." Thanks to the libraries and archives that provided me with materials, especially the Montana Room at the Parmly Billings Library, the Carbon County Historical Society, the Montana State University–Billings Library, and Jodie Moore and Bob Moran at the Red Lodge Carnegie Library. In fact, thanks to everyone in Red Lodge and across Montana and the West: for me, the key to fulfillment is to live in a wonderful community, to love that community, and to write about it. That's what I've tried to do for twenty-three years, and yet it is the existence and support of the community that makes it possible.

Finally, special thanks to my wife, Kari. In addition to taking photographs and developing graphics, she was my best editor, the kind who writes "boring!" in the margins of sections that need to be deleted. And without her healing power, I literally would not have had the strength to complete this book. Nobody can appreciate as much as Kari that the "literally" in that sentence is no mere intensifier.

Index

A

African Americans 48–52, 119
Altyn, Montana. *See* Swift Current, Montana
Anaconda Copper Mining Company 83, 86, 87
authenticity 126–142, 147

B

Baker, Gerard 157–164
Bearcreek, Montana 62, 63, 65, 90–96
Beartooth Highway 62–69
Belle Fourche, South Dakota 42, 43, 44, 45
Bertram, James 26
Bighorn Canyon 13–19, 125–130
Big Timber, Montana 25, 27, 30
Billings, Montana 39–40, 43, 48–52, 78–79, 82–83, 149, 165, 166
Black Bird, Alfred 48–52
Boggio, Kerri 134
Boyd, William 136
Bozeman, Montana 29–30, 35, 37, 85
Brownell, Baker 85
Busch, Jean 132, 134
Butte, Montana 35, 37, 38, 40

C

Camp Senia 55–61, 56, 58, 59
capitalism and capitalists 107, 108
Carnegie, Andrew 24
Cassidy, Butch (Robert Leroy Parker) 42, 44
Cassidy, Hopalong. *See* Hopalong Cassidy (fictional character)
Chinook, Montana 27, 30
class 58, 80, 142, 154
Cody, William F. "Buffalo Bill" 139, 141, 147, 149
Cody, Wyoming 49, 64, 68, 148–149, 152
Cok, Mike 30
Columbus, Montana 38, 39, 43, 66
community 73, 80–81, 84–89, 98, 121, 133, 167
condylarth 95
Conrad, Montana 86, 87
Cooke City, Montana 64–68
Coxey's Army 35–41
Cox, Haydie. *See* Yates, Emma Hayden "Haydie"

Croonquist, Al and Senia 56–61
Currie, George "Flat Nose" 44
Custer, General George A 157

D

Darby, Montana 87
DeVille, Frank 90–93
Dillon, Montana 26, 27, 30
Disney 106, 107
dudes (dude ranch guests) 55–61, 152–156
dudines (dude ranch guests) 152, 153, 154

E

ecotourism 106, 107, 122
Edgar, Montana 49, 51

F

Fahrenthold, Jerry 133
Ferguson, Gary 109–111
Finley, Chris 125–130
Finn, J.D. 38, 40
Forsyth, Montana 40
Fort Benton, Montana 30, 40
fossils 93–95
frontier 55, 59, 82, 84, 106–111, 142, 166
 definition 103, 105
Fuchs, Threse 92

G

Garden of Eden 90, 93–96
Gardiner, Montana 97
gender 71, 150, 153, 154
Gillette, Edward 13, 14, 16
Glacier National Park 22, 70, 72
Glasgow, Montana 27
government 36, 65, 89, 98, 108, 137
Great Falls, Montana 22, 27
Griffin, Walter Burley 80, 81, 83

H

Hamilton, Montana 24, 26, 30
Hardin, Montana 30
Harley Davidson motorcycles 115–117
Haste, Gwendolen 82, 83
Havre, Montana 27, 28
Hawks Rest, Wyoming 109–111
Hogan, William 37, 38
homesteading 77, 82, 105, 126
Hopalong Cassidy (fictional character) 136
Howard, Joseph Kinsey 77, 85

I

independence. *See* individualism
Indians. *See* Native Americans
individualism 98, 121, 133, 137, 152, 163, 169

J

Johnston, John "Liver-eating" 51, 145–149

K

Kalispell, Montana 28
Kid Curry 44, 47
Kid, Sundance. *See* Sundance Kid
Kuralt, Charles 65

L

Langstaff, Gloria 24
Lavina, Montana 43, 45, 46
Lewis, Kate 30
Lewistown, Montana 26, 30, 87
Libby, Montana 88
libraries, Carnegie 24–31
Little Bighorn Battlefield 157–161
Livingston, Montana 27, 30, 38
Lockhart, Caroline 9, 13, 49–52, 71, 119, 125–128, 139
Lodge Grass Creek, Montana 150–156
Logan, Harvey. *See* Kid Curry
Lonepine, Montana 85, 87

INDEX

Longabaugh, Harry. *See* Sundance Kid
Lose, Ann 92

M

Malta, Montana 30
Meadows, Paul 85
Melby, Ernest 85
Miles City, Montana 27, 40, 43
mining 37, 42, 55, 62–66, 70–73, 90–93, 106, 115, 122
Missoula, Montana 27, 28, 86
Montana Study, The 84–89
Mossmain, Montana 77–83
Moss, Preston B. 78–83
mountain man 145, 147
  rendezvous gatherings 131–135
Mulford, Clarence E. 136–138
Munson, Jill 30

N

Native Americans 51, 146, 155, 157–164
New West 115–122
nostalgia 22, 57, 87, 103, 139

O

Old West—And New (Lockhart) 118, 120
Oyler, Mark and Tana 30

P

paleontology 93–96
Parker, Robert Leroy. *See* Cassidy, Butch
Pollari, Senia. *See* Croonquist, Al and Senia
Poston, Richard 87, 88
Propst, Luther 86
Putney, Walt 43–44, 47

R

racial issues. *See* Native Americans, African Americans
Racicot, Marc 88, 89
Red Lodge, Montana 27, 30, 42–47, 55–69, 96, 131–135, 148

rendezvous gatherings. *See* mountain man
Robinson, Tri 148–149
romanticism 55, 57, 87, 107, 111, 119, 132, 142
Russell, Charles M. 20–23

S

Schaffer, Glenn 165, 166, 169
Shanks, Greg 16
Shelley, Oliver H.P. 62, 66, 69
Shirilla, Kathleen 28
Siegfriedt, Dr. J.C.F. 62–66, 93–96
Slonaker, Dick 30
Small Town Renaissance (nonfiction book) 87, 88
Smith, John L. "Red Eye" 48–52
Snow, Don 86, 168
Stevensville, Montana 87
Sundance Kid 45, 47
Suzette (pen name) 70–73
Swift Current, Montana 70–73

T

trapping 48, 107, 131, 134, 145, 148
Turner, Frederick Jackson 103

V

Virginian, The (Wister) 103, 119, 169

W

Whitney, Gertrude Vanderbilt 139–141
Wister, Owen 56, 103, 119, 169
women. *See* gender

Y

Yates, Emma Hayden "Haydie" 150–156
Yellowstone Bighorn Research Association 95
Yellowstone National Park 7, 68, 106, 109

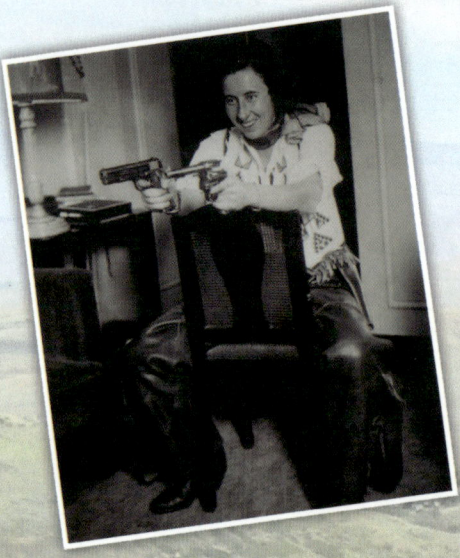

WHEN MONTANA RAN OUT OF FRONTIER, ITS UNIQUE HISTORY REALLY BEGAN.

At the turn of the twentieth century, Montana started emerging from its rugged past. Permanent towns and cities, powered by mining, tourism, and trade, replaced ramshackle outposts. Yet Montana's frontier endured, both in remote pockets and in the wider cultural imagination. The frontier thus played a continuing role in Montanans' lives, often in fascinating ways. Author John Clayton has written extensively on these shifts in Montana history, chronicling the breadth of the frontier's legacy with this diverse collection of stories. Explore the remnants of Montana's frontier through stories of the Little Bighorn Battlefield, the Beartooth Highway, and the lost mining camp of Swift Current—and through legendary characters such as Charlie Russell, Haydie Yates, and "Liver-eating" Johnston.

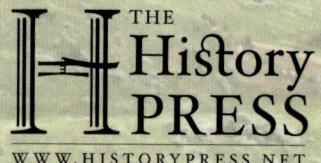

$19.99

ISBN 978-1-62619-016-0